WINNERS

THE WILL TO DO, THE SOUL TO DARE
Sir Walter Scott

University of Winnipeg, 515 Portage Ave., Winnipeg, MB   R3B 2E9 Canada

WINNERS

A Century of Canadian Sport

Published by

Grosvenor House TORONTO/ MONTREAL

and

The Canadian Press

The publishers wish to acknowledge the assistance of
(M) Molson Breweries of Canada Limited
in the publication of this book.

Canadian Cataloguing in Publication Data

Main entry under title:
Winners : a century of Canadian sport

Published also in French under title: Les
étoiles : un siècle de sport au Canada.
ISBN 0-919959-22-9

1. Sport—Canada—Addresses, essays, lectures.
2. Sport—Canada—History—Addresses, essays,
lectures. I. Canadian Press.

GV585.W55 1985   796'.0971   C85-099733-X

Published by

Grosvenor House Press Inc.
111 Queen St. East
Suite 375
Toronto, Ontario, Canada
M5C 1S2

Éditions Grosvenor Inc.
1456, rue Sherbrooke ouest
3ᵉ étage
Montréal, Québec, Canada
H3G 1K4

The Canadian Press
36 King St. East
Toronto, Ontario, Canada
M5C 2L9

La Presse Canadienne
245 ouest rue St. Jacques
Montréal, Québec, Canada
H2Y 3J6

Printed and bound in Canada
Cover design by David Sutherland
Page design by Bob Paul

Table of Contents

Introduction

To challenge limits is a human instinct as old as the will to survive. Whether in competition against others, or against barriers of time, height, distance, speed, weight, territory or environment, succeeding generations have always striven to exceed the marks set by their predecessors. Unflinching commitment, determination of steel, and a driving will to win are the hallmarks of champions, those who make the leap from being good to becoming THE BEST at what they do.

This book is a tribute to those who have excelled in one particular field — sports. It is a salute to the winners who have left their marks in the records of Canadian sports. Many of the stories are well known to every sports fan in Canada — Paul Henderson's goal that September in Moscow, the elation of Alex Baumann in the pool in Los Angeles, and the dazzling brilliance and tragic death of Gilles Villeneuve. Other stories are remembered by very few — the impish Ned Hanlan, Canada's 1936 hockey loss to England and the Canadian who invented basketball. And some stories are not yet complete — how many more times will the record books be rewritten by Number 99? And will 1986 be the year that Canadians finally recognize the amazing accomplishments of Rick Hansen?

They are just a few of the countless thousands who are winners at every level of sport, from professional to sandlot. On our 200th anniversary, Molson proudly salutes not only the winners but all who participate in sports of every kind. It is a privilege to be associated with those who strive to excel and who have the desire to challenge their own abilities, for these are the same qualities that for 200 years have guided Molson people. Most of all, in celebrating this milestone in our history, we pay sincere tribute to the millions of Canadians in communities, clubs and organizations across Canada, with whom we have the pleasure of being associated through promotions, sponsorships and the simple sharing of good times.

It is to Canadian sports participants, enthusiasts and fans that we dedicate this book.

Molson Breweries of Canada Limited 1786–1986

Celebrating 200 years of excellence

Ned Hanlan

THE FIRST CHAMPION OF THE WORLD
BY GEOFF FRASER
THE CANADIAN PRESS, TORONTO

The year was 1880, and rowing was the rage of the English-speaking world when Ned Hanlan, a young Toronto oarsman, brought fame to Canada. A twenty-five-year-old slip of a man, standing five-foot-eight and weighing 155 pounds, Hanlan spent his youth in a makeshift shell he had built on his own, teaching himself to be an oarsman, in the waters of Toronto Harbor.

Hanlan competed in his first professional race at age nineteen and won. Five years later, he had won the U.S. Centennial International regatta and was Canadian, U.S. and British champion. "The Boy in Blue," as the international press came to call him because of his characteristic racing attire of blue jersey and blue shorts, was the sensation of the rowing world. He was also a hero to the public who had fallen in love with this small, handsome man who so easily beat his bigger, stronger opponents.

On November 15, 1880, Hanlan's fame in the history of international sports was enshrined. The Canadian had challenged Edward Trickett, a hulk of an Australian who claimed to be champion of the world after beating the number 1 British rower. As no other sport then in existence boasted a world champion, it was a novel claim. But because Trickett would not compete in North America, the rowing establishment—and public—would not accept his title.

When Hanlan and Trickett finally met that fateful November afternoon on the River Thames in London to decide the issue, the British press called the match "the event of the century in rowing." When the inevitable morning fog finally dissipated, more than 100,000 spectators could be seen lining the four-mile, 440-yard course.

Trickett was huge—six-foot-four, 210 pounds — and his backers, the Thompson brothers of Sydney, Aus-

tralia, were so confident of victory, they bet New York bookmakers to a standstill. One estimate put the amount wagered on the race at almost $500,000—an incredible sum one hundred years ago.

The race started next to the Star and Garter Hotel. Trickett, who appeared anxious, won the toss and picked the right hand side of the river. Hanlan, however, was playful as he bantered with officials, "and he did not look as though embarking on a race concerning which so many interests were at stake," related William E. Harding, sports editor of the *Police Gazette* of New York.

At 12:14 p.m., the two oarsmen broke the starting line. Hanlan used 35 strokes to the minute, Trickett stroked 40. But Trickett never had the ghost of a chance. Within the first mile, Hanlan had a two-length lead. His long, clean, efficient strokes were destroying the Australian.

The real race was over in the first mile. What followed was typical Hanlan gamesmanship. "He treated the onlookers to a dose of those remarkable manoeuvres which created such intense astonishment," said Harding. "Hanlan . . . made sport of him (Trickett) and played monkey

capers all over the river in a race which decided more money than ever rowed in the world."

Hanlan "lay back in his shell with the most perfect nonchalance, lazily paddling first with one scull and then the other," described *The Canadian Illustrated News*. The young Canadian waved to the crowd, stretched, and even pretended to stop for a drink of water from the river while Trickett strained to catch up.

Then halfway through the race Hanlan showed a "piece of harlequinade, the like of which was never witnessed in a race. Dropping his sculls clumsily into the water, he fell right forward upon his face and lay there for a second or two. So long did he remain in a recumbent position that a kind of groan came from the spectators, who imagined something terrible had befallen him. But before they could find their voices to shout and inquire what was the matter, he sprung up, suddenly resumed the sculls, and was at work again, laughing merrily." The final margin of victory was judged at three lengths, but it could easily have been 30. "Hanlan's victories over oarsmen who were in many aspects his superior physically have created universal wonder and surprise," wrote Harding. "The secret is Hanlan is one of the most finished scullers that ever sat in a shell."

Hanlan defended his world professional crown six times before losing to Australian William Beach on the Paramatta River in 1884. By the time Hanlan retired from active competition in 1897, he had competed in more than 300 races. Records exist for six defeats.

On January 4, 1908, Toronto mourned the death of its twice-elected alderman and famous "Boy in Blue."

James Naismith
THE NEW GAME
BY GRAHAM COX
THE CANADIAN PRESS, OTTAWA

You have to go a long way from his Canadian birthplace to find out much about James Naismith. In fact, except for a plaque at the Canadian Sports Hall of Fame in Toronto and a few brief mentions in sports anthologies, you'd have to go to Springfield, Massachusetts, to find out that this unassuming theologian, athlete and academic created the game of basketball. But, then, Naismith always was modest about creating what is said to be the most popular sport in the world.

Naismith developed the game at the request of Dr. Luther Gulick, physical education director of Springfield College where he was teaching clean living through sport. The first game of what has been called "the first deliberately invented sport" was played there in 1891, with a soccer ball and two peach baskets attached at either end of the school gymnasium.

Although he coached the game until his retirement as head of physical education at the University of Kansas in Lawrence in 1937, winning was never Naismith's aim. In fact, he was more interested in the academic side of life, acquiring eleven university degrees in such areas as theology, medicine and physical education. But he never practised as a doctor and he never held a pastoral charge, preferring to minister to his charges through sport.

Naismith died in Lawrence, Kansas, in 1939. And, although he was born about forty kilometres west of Ottawa on a farm near Almonte, Ontario on November 6, 1861, and took his arts and divinity degrees at McGill and the Presbyterian Theological College in Montreal, his

memory is best preserved at Springfield, site of the Basketball Hall of Fame.

There is a school named after him at Almonte, but there isn't even a roadside plaque at the farm where he was born and raised, nor at Bennie's Corners where he attended school. In fact, while the house he was raised in still stands, all the memorabilia from his time there remain packed away in boxes in the basements of relatives of Edna Lowry who was still trying to interest someone in a Naismith museum in Almonte when she died recently at eighty-nine.

But this strongly dedicated man with his stern Scots Presbyterian upbringing would probably have brushed off any adulation as unwarranted. In answer to one section of a questionnaire sent with his application to McGill in 1888, Naismith said that the sweetest words he could ever hear would be: "You've been a great help to me."

The Mighty Men of Zorra

BY BRUCE LEVETT
THE CANADIAN PRESS, TORONTO

They were all farmers and they were all neighbors from the township of Zorra. They lived within walking distance of the tiny centre of Embro, Ontario, and their heritage was Scottish. Embro was the Gaelic word for Edinburgh, and they were all the sons of highlanders. Their names were Alex Clark, William B. Munro, Robert McLeod, Ira Hummason, Robert McIntosh and Ebenezer L. (Little Abe) Sutherland. They were the Mighty Men of Zorra and, in 1893, were recognized as the greatest tug of war team in the world.

Tug of war? That funny sport engaged in by the volunteer fire department at the Canada Day picnic? That's the one, son, but back then it was taken super-seriously. In fact, it was an Olympic Games sport from 1900 to 1920. When the Zorras took the world title nearly one hundred years ago at the Chicago World's Fair, they had to defeat twenty-three countries to do it.

The Zorras weren't all that serious about the sport when they first got into it. But all the other townships in southwestern Ontario had teams, so these brawny men asked themselves "Why not?" By 1888 they had wiped out Canadian competition and had gone international. They pulled their last match on July 4, 1893—the day they beat the world.

Except in strength and spirit, these men were not giants. McIntosh, the anchorman, was the biggest at six-foot-two, 215 pounds. Munro, the smallest, was six-foot-one, 188 pounds.

Nor were they young men, by 1893. They averaged forty-five years of age. Hummason was an amazing fifty-one at the time of that championship pull, and he was considered the strongest of them all. Stories survive of him hoisting two 115-pound anvils, one in each hand, at arm's length. McIntosh, the legends have it, could hold two heavy draught horses once he got set into position.

And maybe position had a lot to do with the Zorras' success. Their form was to dig their boots into the ground, inches deep, and lie back. In tug of war, a flag is tied in the centre of the rope and the ground is marked with a line two feet on either side of the flag. The object is to pull the flag over the line on your side.

Unlike today's athletes, the Zorras didn't really train—they didn't need to. Each man had cleared five acres of timber with his axe that year, then cut the wood into stove lengths. They were grain farmers, and oats were bringing seventeen cents a bushel. To get the grain to the mill, they carried it—on their shoulders, in two-bushel bags. Each bag weighed 120 pounds and the mill was thirteen miles away, down a trail through the forest.

When the Zorras went international in 1888, they won in a walk, taking the North American crown in Buffalo, New York. They returned to Embro to wild celebrations which led to a rift that could have split the team. "These carryings-on did not please McLeod, the only non-drinker on the team and he is said to have threatened to quit if his mates did not mend their ways," one account has it. In future, McLeod was in charge of the team refreshments.

Meanwhile, two years had passed and Chicago had produced a mighty opponent. In August 1890, this team challenged the Zorras for the title and beat them. The sports world reeled, and skulduggery was suggested because the Chicago hosts had not allowed McIntosh to wear his anchor belt.

Zorra demanded a rematch on their own ground and got it—October 10, 1890. They took the first heat of the three-heat affair in less than a minute. Heat two, however, was a different story. For a full 25 minutes, the two teams lay like rocks, their muscles straining. Suddenly, a piper

began to skirl and the sons of high-landers responded. When it was over, after 35 minutes of "action", the two teams lay exhausted. Zorra had won but, as a contemporary report states, "gentle and willing hands carefully pried fingers, one by one, from their death grip on the rope."

Three years later, when the world competition was held, Zorra met Chicago again for all the marbles. Again, the hosts disputed the use of a belt by McIntosh, offering instead a lighter model such as they wore. The upshot was that neither anchor-man wore a belt, but curled the rope around his unprotected waist to take the slack.

Again, the contest was best-of-three. The first heat went to Zorra in six minutes. For the second heat, the venue was changed to the opposite corner of the field where the hot sun shone in the visitors' eyes and the baked ground prevented them from digging in. Chicago averaged 25 pounds per man weight advantage and they wiped out the Zorras in two minutes.

For heat three, the championship round, the killing ground was moved again. This time they braced up in front of the grandstand "on black earth, where a westering sun cast a shadow." The Zorras fell into their familiar position and dug in. Chicago also rammed home their heels and took up the slack. They strained motionless and this time there was no piper there to raise the Scottish spirits.

Little Abe studied the Chicago faces for signs of weakness and, suddenly, called, "NOW—all togeth-er. . ." The ribbon moved and, slowly, kept on moving. The crowd erupted onto the field to cheer the Mighty Men of Zorra. The time of that last pull was not recorded.

Tommy Burns
THE NEGLECTED CANADIAN CHAMPION
BY MILT DUNNELL
THE TORONTO STAR

Pound for pound, the best heavy-weight champion of *this century* almost certainly was Noah Brusso, alias Tommy Burns, the little lacrosse player from Hanover, Ontario. But make that statement in your favorite bar and you will probably be forced into Muhammad Ali's peek-a-boo defence in order to escape a technical knockout.

Although he was the only Cana-dian ever to hold the heavyweight title, Tommy Burns never received the credit he deserved, even from Canadians. Most boxing fans pre-ferred to consider him a caretaker champion, who held the title while the fight world sorted out a logical successor to James J. Jeffries, the beloved Boilermaker, who had re-tired in May 1905 because he had run out of worthy opponents. The fact that Burns did not earn the title by defeating Jeffries in the ring made him a jerry-built champion in the eyes of most fight fans of the time.

Burns, of course, was never a heavyweight physically. He was a legitimate light heavyweight who disdained that unpopular fistic divi-sion. Only five foot seven inches in height, he weighed 172 pounds when he launched his campaign to become the successor to Jeffries. Although he got to be as heavy as 183 pounds during one stage of his career, Burns weighed only 168 when he lost the championship to Jack Johnson, the first black to win the title.

There may be those who will argue that Ruby Red Fitzsimmons has to be the greatest heavyweight champion, pound for pound. He weighed only 167 pounds when he took the title from Gentleman Jim Corbett, but it should be remem-bered that the championship bout was not in the twentieth century.

Despite his small stature, Burns was a devastating puncher. His knockout percentage was .600 in 60 professional fights. By comparison, Gene Tunney, twice the conqueror of Jack Dempsey, and probably the most popular heavyweight prior to the Ali era, had a knockout percen-tage of .539 in 76 fights. Dempsey, the famed Manassa Mauler, had a knockout mark of .605 in 81 fights. In other words, statistically speak-ing, Burns keeps good company. It will be argued, and it's true, that Dempsey's opponents, such as Tun-ney, Jack Sharkey and Jess Willard, were much tougher than Marvin Hart, Bill Squires and Big Jem Roche, who were on the Burns hit list. But Burns fought the people who were available. After all, there are names on Dempsey's roster that are not exactly engraved in the annals of boxing. Who remembers Porky Flynn, Fred Saddy or Kid Henry?

Burns's knockout of Jem Roche, in Dublin, on St. Patrick's Day, remains in the record book as the quickest undisputed heavyweight title knockout in history. The time was 1:28 of the first round. In the infamous fiasco between Cassius Clay (Muhammad Ali) and Sonny Liston, at Lewiston, Maine, in May 1965, Clay was credited with starch-ing Liston, with a phantom punch, in one minute flat. Like everything else about that non-fight, though, the time of the knockout was ques-tioned later. Stop-watches synchro-nized with television film frames of the event caught Liston doing his dive at 1:42 and Joe Walcott, the

referee, ending the charade at 2:12. There was no such dispute concerning the Burns knockout of Roche.

Why a young Canadian lacrosse player, actually too small for the heavyweight division, would aspire to follow in the ring-prints of giants like John Sullivan and Jim Jeffries, is almost as puzzling as the question of Burns's origins. He is listed in The Ring, the bible of boxing, as French-Canadian. He was also billed as an Italian-Canadian, but it must be taken into consideration that fight promoters felt free to meddle with a fighter's nationality if it spurred the sale of tickets.

Burns himself said he was of German extraction and that he had been raised in the Methodist faith. A plaque erected by the Ontario Archeological and Historical Site Board, near the fairgrounds at Hanover in 1959, gives the year of his birth as 1881 (actual date, June 17). The twelfth of thirteen children of Frederick and Sofa Brusso, who lived in Normandy Township, Burns recalled in later years that he left the Handen school, a few miles from Hanover, when he was ten years old, and that he then could lick any kid on the school grounds.

Burns gave at least two versions of his reasons for turning to fist fighting. In one, he was playing lacrosse for a Detroit team, when a sports editor there, impressed by his muscles, asked whether he had ever considered boxing. Burns (still named Brusso) liked the idea, so the editor introduced him to a promoter friend.

A more colorful version, possibly the product of a press agent, had Burns working as a baggage handler on a lake boat that operated between Buffalo and Cleveland. The second engineer on the boat was a self-styled tough guy who had earned his reputation by intimidating new hands. When he tried to push Brusso around, he discovered he had been overmatched and took refuge in his cabin. The other crew members were so impressed that they insisted their new champion should take up boxing.

Regardless of which story — if either — is factual, Brusso did join the Detroit Athletic Club and go into training. His first fight of record was at Detroit in 1900 and it apparently came about by accident. He and a party of friends had gone to see a boxing match between Jack Cowan and a local favorite named Fred Thornton, but Cowan slipped and twisted an ankle while climbing into the ring.

Brusso's friends conned him into bailing out Mike Dolan, the promoter, by taking on Thornton. Brusso was willing but Thornton was apprehensive, finally agreeing only if Brusso signed an agreement exonerating Thornton in case he killed the brash Canadian.

Brusso knocked out Thornton in five rounds. The grateful Dolan asked how much Brusso expected for the fight. "Enough to buy the boys a cigar or two," Brusso told him. Dolan handed him $1.25. It was the first of many small pay days for the future champion, whose career earnings were $208,954.25, which, in those times, sounded like a lot of money.

After the debut with Thornton, Brusso went on to become the middleweight champion of Michigan. He and his handlers spent a night in jail after Burns gave a fighter named Ben O'Grady a severe beating. O'Grady was unconscious for three days, and Burns was charged with assault. Because his mother became distressed over the publicity surrounding that incident, Brusso adopted the ring name of Tommy Burns.

When Jeffries announced his intention to retire, Burns, who had always acted as his own manager, was quick to appreciate the implications. He decided he was going to be the new champion. But Tommy Ryan, a friend of Jeffries and a wily old fight manager, also realized the possibilities. Jeffries had seen one of Ryan's fighters named Marvin Hart in action and was impressed. At Ryan's urging, Jeffries indicated he would recognize Hart as champion if Hart could defeat a suitable opponent.

The opponent was Jack Root of Chicago. Jeffries refereed the fight which was held in Reno but, although Hart knocked out Root, he received practically no acceptance as the new champion. Certainly, he was not recognized by Burns, who in February 1906, beat Hart in 20 rounds at Los Angeles and claimed the title. But he, too, received little recognition until he defeated Philadelphia Jack O'Brien.

In his warmup campaign for O'Brien, Burns fought two men — Jim O'Brien and Jim Walker, on the same night, March 28, 1906, and knocked out both of them in the first round. Then he knocked out Jim Flynn in the fifteenth round of a bout that was given championship recognition — with Burns as the defender.

That brought on Philadelphia Jack O'Brien. With Jeffries as referee the first fight ended in a draw. O'Brien used the draw as an excuse to claim the title but no one was paying attention, so it was agreed they should fight again. If, at the end of 20 rounds, Jeffries, who was again the referee, decided it was an even fight, he would demand extra rounds. There had to be a winner. This time, Burns won in the regular distance.

Now, with general acceptance as the heavyweight champion of the world, Burns declared himself ready to fight anybody who could provide a decent pay day. Gunner Moir was the English champion and Burns's first stop was London. A match was made for the National Sporting Club in London on December 2, 1907.

After getting a sneak preview of the English champion, Burns went out and wagered 400 pounds on himself to win. Burns knocked out Moir in the tenth round before a fashionable audience that included King Edward VII and immediately became a favorite of the fight set, who entertained him lavishly in England and on the Continent.

In Dublin, Burns knocked out Jem Roche, the Irish champion, with one punch. Next, he flattened Australian Bill Squires in Paris. He and Squires then departed for Australia, seeking more pay days. In Australia, Burns knocked out Squires for the third time, in a match at Sydney, then moved on to Melbourne where he flattened Bill Lang, another Australian.

Meanwhile, Jack Johnson had been on his trail, clamoring for a shot at the title which he had been unable to get in North America. But Johnson was black and the United States was not ready for a black heavyweight champion. The mighty John L. Sullivan had spelled out the mood of the times in the famous challenge which he issued through The Associated Press, on March 5, 1892: "I hereby challenge one and all of the bluffers who have been trying to make capital at my expense, to fight me, either the last week of August, this year, or the first week of September, this year, at the Olympic Club in New Orleans, for a purse of $25,000 and an outside bet of $10,000, the winner to take the entire purse. In this challenge, I include all fighters, first come, first served, who are white. I will not fight a Negro. I never have and never shall."

Burns imposed no color bar, provided the money was to his liking. A London promoter had gained some publicity, at Burns's expense, by offering 3,000 pounds for a fight with Johnson in London. Burns, booed at the famous Wonderland Arena in London because he refused the offer, addressed the crowd and said: "I am my own manager. Now, I put it to you, if you were offered 3,000 pounds for a fight but another promoter offered 6,000 pounds, which would you accept? I know I can get 6,000 pounds and I will fight Jack Johnson."

Burns made good on both the promise and the prediction. He signed, a few months later, with Hugh McIntosh, an Australian promoter, for 6,000 pounds, plus 1,000 pounds for training expenses. The fight took place at the Rushcutter's

Bay Arena, near Sydney, on December 26, 1908. Although Burns was the 3 to 2 favorite in the betting, the fight was an obvious mismatch. Johnson was more than six feet tall and weighed 192 pounds. Burns weighed 168.

The fight could not have been as bad, though, as it was pictured by the famous author Jack London, who covered the fight for the *New York Herald*. Describing it as a contest between a colossus and a pygmy, London wrote that Johnson play-acted through the fight and that Burns never landed a meaningful blow.

It was Burns's misfortune that London's account of the fight was the one that received the widest acceptance and is recalled, even to this day. Few ever ask why, if Burns failed to land a meaningful punch, he was still on his feet in the fourteenth round when the police intervened. Many years later, Nat Fleischer wrote: "After years of study devoted to the heavyweights, I have no hesitation in naming Jack Johnson the greatest of them all . . . He was a fine boxer, a good hitter and a powerful counterpuncher." In retrospect, does it make sense that a man with those qualities would deliberately carry Burns for 14 rounds?

Burns later claimed that London came to him with tears in his eyes, some weeks after the fight, and apologized for what he had written. As Burns put it: "Thanks, but the damage has been done."

In any attempt to reach a realistic appraisal of Burns's stature as a heavyweight champion, heed should be paid to *Ring Magazine*'s ranking of all champions in all divisions. Philadelphia Jack O'Brien was rated the best of all light heavyweight champions. This was the same O'Brien whom Burns had defeated to gain general recognition as heavyweight champion.

After trying his hand at pub ownership in London, and a night-club operation in New York, Burns took on the role of evangelist. John Lardner, a noted American writer, wrote a column for News Week in 1955, in which he recalled that "about halfway through his life, Burns felt what he thought was the touch of the Lord's hand on his shoulder. The change in Tommy's speech and character must have startled men who had known him in the old days."

There is evidence, however, that the touch of the Almighty's hand might have fallen less heavily on Burns's shoulder if he had been able to develop a political career in his native country. In the Canadian Sports Hall of Fame, there is a letter which Burns, who was then living in New York, wrote to R.B. Bennett, then prime minister of Canada, in September 1934. Introducing himself as the former heavyweight champion of the world, Burns made his pitch for a job: "I have been thinking, for some time, of coming to Canada to live—in short, to finish the remainder of my life there—and, if it is possible, I would like to get a government position. The elections are coming up and I believe I would be a great help. Any position you think would suit me would be satisfactory."

Bennett was as cool to Canada's only heavyweight champion as most other Canadians had been for almost three decades. On November 6 of that year, he replied to Burns's letter: "It is a matter of great satisfaction to know you have not lost interest in the affairs of this country, in spite of some years' absence. I propose to keep your letter before me and, should the occasion arise, when your offer of service could be accepted, I will again communicate with you." Needless to say, the occasion did not arise.

This was one of several attempts

by the former champion to re-establish himself in his native land. In partnership with an old lacrosse friend, he had opened a clothing store in Calgary in 1910, but it was unsuccessful.

Burns also tried his hand as a fight promoter, with tragic results. Professional fist fighting was illegal in Calgary at the time, so Tommy built a makeshift wooden arena just outside the zone covered by the prohibitive bylaw. Ever since the shock of Jim Jeffries' failure to beat Jack Johnson, there had been a frantic search among white heavyweights for a man who might take the title from Johnson. Although Burns had refused to observe the ban against blacks when he was champion, he participated in the so-called White Hope hunt. Two of the hopefuls were Arthur Pelkey and Luther McCarty who were matched in Burns's makeshift arena. McCarty collapsed and died after taking a punch to the jaw in the first round. The tragedy created the usual outcry about boxing brutality and it ended Burns's dreams of becoming a big promoter.

After Burns's death on May 10, 1955, many observers of the fight scene reached the belated conclusion that Burns was a much better fighter than he had ever received credit for. John Lardner observed: "He had come down in tradition as one of the minor heavyweight champions but it's likely he was better than anyone who has held the title since Tunney's time, with the exception of Joe Louis and perhaps Rocky Marciano. Burns was not big but he was strong, fast and he could hit."

Burns had been elected to the *Ring Magazine* Boxing Hall of Fame in New York, in 1960, and was a member of the Canadian Sports Hall of Fame. It came as something of a shock, therefore, when it became known, in 1961, that Burns's body lay in an unmarked Canadian grave.

Andy O'Brien, then sports editor of *Weekend Magazine*, had written a column when Burns was named to the International Hall of Fame. When Fred (Cyclone) Taylor, one of hockey's all-time greats, read the column, he began inquiring about the location of Burns's grave. Taylor, who had played lacrosse against Burns when he was known as Noah Brusso, learned to his surprise that Burns had been buried in British Columbia. "I rounded up three old-time Vancouver lacrosse players to help me locate the grave," Taylor wrote to O'Brien. "Tommy lies in an unmarked patch of grass. We have pledged to raise a fund for a grave marker."

Nat Fleischer, boxing's most famous historian, had already provided a paragraph that would have made a fitting epitaph for a monument to Canada's long neglected and underestimated sports hero: "He was the only champion who was forced to dispose of every title claimant, in every land where boxing was followed, before he received international recognition as possessor of the world heavyweight crown."

Right: Tommy Burns

The Klondikers' Odyssey

BY LAURIE STEPHENS
THE CANADIAN PRESS, TORONTO

In 1905, before the days of the National Hockey League, eight men from the Frozen North travelled 7,000 kilometres to challenge a mighty Ottawa team for hockey supremacy. It was a determined odyssey by a very determined group of hockey players.

From Dawson City, Yukon, to Skagway, Alaska, they trekked, carting their equipment on dogsleds. They lost a whole day's travelling time when they missed their boat to Vancouver by two hours and had to wait five days for another to Seattle. From Seattle, they travelled by train to Vancouver and then on to Ottawa, arriving one day before the first of two games with the famed Ottawa Silver Seven, holders of the Stanley Cup.

The challenge was sponsored by Colonel Joe Boyle, a wealthy, eccentric prospector who was convinced that his team would sweep the Ottawans off their feet. After all, the eight men selected to the team — centre Hector Smith, forward George (Sureshot) Kennedy, point Jim Johnson, spare Archie Martin, cover-point (defenceman) Randy McLennan, forward Norman Watts, rover Dave Fairburn and goaltender Albert Forrest — had all played hockey on eastern clubs before moving to Dawson City. To counter the absence of team captain Weldy Young, who was tied up with business, cover-point Lorne Hannay of Brandon was recruited on the way to Ottawa.

The team set out on their expedition in December, 1905, with high hopes. "The all-star hockey team that is to go east and battle for the Stanley Cup and, incidentally, show some of the oldtime cracks how the noble game should be played, expects to get away either today or Sunday," the *Yukon World* reported on December 17.

Twenty-six days later, after enduring cramped quarters and little exercise during the latter part of the journey, the Klondikers arrived in Ottawa amid great fanfare. Forrest, Dawson's seventeen-year-old goaltender, sent the *Yukon World* a telegram that was printed on January 13: "We arrived safely yesterday and had a good, full practice on the rink today. As the Ottawa team has refused postponement, we play the first game tomorrow night. Enormous interest is shown in our trip throughout the whole country and big excitement in Ottawa."

More than 2,200 hockey fans, including Canada's Governor-General Earl Grey, and his wife, packed the stands to watch the Silver Seven defend the Stanley Cup title for the eighth time in four years.

From the moment the Klondikers stepped on the ice, though, they were hopelessly outclassed. The team of tired, aging players was outskated, outmuscled and outscored 9–2 in the rough opening contest.

Still, there was optimism going into the second game, as reported on January 14 in the Yukon paper: "It is realized that with two days more practice and a recovery from the long journey, the Klondikers team will have an excellent chance. The betting is only slightly in favor of the Ottawas."

So much for optimism. The Klondikers were humiliated 23–2 in a game noteworthy only because of the 14-goal splurge by the one-eyed Ottawa forward, Willie McGee. Colonel Boyle's $3,000 investment was a bust, and the Dawson City Klondikers, after completing a series of exhibition games against lesser teams, returned home, never to be heard from in the East again.

Below: The Klondikers in Dawson City

Sir Barton

BY JIM COLEMAN

When Sir Barton, owned by Commander J.K.L. Ross of Montreal, became the first horse to win the Kentucky Derby, the Preakness Stakes and the Belmont Stakes in 1919, racing fans did not immediately realize just what this great horse had accomplished — a precedent-setting series of racing triumphs of historic importance. For it wasn't until twenty years later that the Derby, the Preakness and the Belmont were officially designated as "The Triple Crown" of North American racing and a trophy was awarded to the owner of the horse which won all three.

Commander Ross was North America's leading owner of thoroughbreds from 1919 through 1923 when his horses were trained by the celebrated H. Guy Bedwell. The inheritor of considerable money from his father who was one of the builders of the Canadian Pacific Railway, Ross's racing fortunes were at their peak in August 1918, when the Montrealer spent $10,000 to acquire a winless two-year-old, Sir Barton, from owner-breeder John E. Madden.

Although he had raced respectably against the best two-year-olds in America, Sir Barton was still a non-winner when he was entered at Churchill Downs to be the pace-setter for his more celebrated stable-mate, Billy Kelly. When Earl Sande, who was the contract-jockey for the Ross Stable, was given his choice of mounts, he selected Billy Kelly, and Johnny Loftus was thereupon assigned to ride the more lightly regarded Sir Barton.

The Derby was raced on May 10, 1919, on a very muddy track. When the starter sent the twelve colts on their way, Sir Barton rushed into a handy lead; he set his own pace for the entire run of one mile and one-quarter, and he won easily, with Billy Kelly finishing second, five lengths behind him.

It was only four days later when Sir Barton won the Preakness Stakes at Baltimore. He was then shipped to New York where he won the Withers Stakes on May 24. Two weeks later, Commander Ross's all-conquering colt won the Belmont Stakes. For this feat as the first Triple Crown champion, Sir Barton would gain posthumous recognition.

A royally bred colt with exceptional ability and a thoroughly irascible disposition, Sir Barton had the misfortune to be supported by tender, "shelly" feet which probably shortened his racing career. Although shod very carefully by A.S. Dodd, the Ross Stable blacksmith, in one race the colt lost all four shoes.

Nevertheless, Sir Barton established himself clearly as the best three-year-old in America. In that 1919 season, he won eight of his thirteen starts; he finished second three times and third in his other two races. Weight never bothered him — he carried 133 pounds in winning the Maryland Handicap.

The Ross Stable, with Sir Barton contributing five victories, had another successful season in 1920 but a bright new star, Man o' War, appeared in the racing firmament. Man o' War has generally been recognized as the greatest thoroughbred of the first half of this century and, after he disposed easily of his three-year-old rivals, there was a general clamor for a match-race against the older Sir Barton.

The successful bidder for "The Race of the Century" was A.M. Orpen of Toronto, who operated Kenilworth Park at Windsor, Ontario. The match was set for October 12, 1920, at a distance of one mile and one-quarter with a winner-take-all purse of $80,000. Regrettably, the historic event proved to be a sorry

mismatch — the younger, bigger Man o' War led from flagfall to finish and Sir Barton was beaten handily by seven lengths.

Man o' War was retired to stud immediately. Sir Barton went to the post three more times in 1920, but he was second twice and third once, in stakes company. Although one of the greatest racehorses of his time, Sir Barton's final years were not illustrious. At the stud farm, he was a disaster, failing to sire any horses of distinction. Before he died in 1937, he suffered the final ignominy of being forced to stand at a United States cavalry remount farm, where his stud fee was a contemptible ten dollars.

The Bluenose
THE FASTEST SALTBANKER AFLOAT
BY ALAN ADAMS
THE CANADIAN PRESS, HALIFAX

"She was as fast as a barracuda," says Claude Darrach, who as a teenage fisherman was invited to sail on the sleek schooner that was to prove the fastest saltbanker of the North American fleet.

Now in his eighties and living in Halifax, Darrach recalls that at its launching in March 1921, the 44-metre speedster, christened the Bluenose, swung steadily away from Lunenburg's Smith and Rhuland shipyard until the bow pointed seaward. According to marine folklore, it was a good omen for a newly launched ship. And so it proved to

be, as the Bluenose turned her tail on all challengers, winning an unparallelled string of victories against the Canadian and American schooners built to fish Atlantic cod.

At the end of her first fishing season on the Grand Banks, the Bluenose returned to port where the hull was cleaned of barnacles and seaweed, and the working booms and fishing sails removed, in preparation for the Nova Scotia Fleet Race. At stake was the right to represent Canada in its effort to wrest the International Fishermen's Trophy from the Americans, who had won it the

Left: The Bluenose

Centre: The Elsie

Right: The Bluenose

year before with the Esperanto of Gloucester, Massachusetts.

This was a time when fishermen looked with scorn at the blue-blood yachts of the America's Cup races being held off Newport, Rhode Island. To qualify for the Fishermen's Trophy, put up by W.H. Dennis, publisher of the *Halifax Herald*, a vessel had to be a saltbanker with at least one season on the Grand Banks.

Built by Nova Scotia craftsmen of spruce, oak and birch, with masts of Oregon pine, the Bluenose easily won the Canadian eliminations. The graceful schooner was then ready to go for the trophy under the command of the tough Angus Walters.

Elsie, skippered by Marty Welch who lived in Digby, Nova Scotia, but who sailed out of Gloucester,

was chosen to defend the title after the Esperanto split in two on a submerged wreck off treacherous Sable Island in May 1921. It had been the Elsie that had picked up the Esperanto's crew and landed them at Halifax.

The first race in the best-of-three series was held on October 22, 1921. Excitement ran high among the crowd at Halifax's Point Pleasant Park where, in earlier days, crows and seabirds had pecked at the bodies of mutineers and other criminals swinging from the gibbets.

The Elsie got off to a fast start but Walters sailed through Elsie's lee and forced her into calmer waters. The Bluenose was almost two minutes ahead at the first mark on the 63-kilometre course but the determined American boat fought back. With canvas straining in the stiffening breeze, the schooners flew down the nine kilometres to the second marker and rounded the buoy with the Bluenose only seconds ahead. "We could have chewed tobacco together," Darrach recalls.

The Bluenose and Elsie went almost bow-to-bow to the third and fourth legs but the Bluenose pulled away on the homeward stretch. With seas plunging over the bow, Walters raised his ballooner and the Bluenose responded like a greyhound, galloping home almost thirteen minutes ahead of the Elsie. Welch followed suit but when he set his ballooner, the wind carried away his foretopmast.

After the race, a Bluenose crew member ran into the wife of the Elsie's captain, who had watched the contest from a Halifax pier. "Well now, Mrs. Welch, it's a pity the Elsie didn't win the race," the fisherman drawled. "And you know, Elsie would've won if it weren't for something in the water today." "Really? What was in the water?" asked the woman. "The Bluenose," he replied.

"There was no vessel that could match her," said Darrach. "The Elsie had no chance. If they'd had a boat that equalled the Bluenose, it would have been a good race."

The second race was held two days later but the story was practically the same. "We were never worried," says Darrach. "The Elsie never had a chance."

The Elsie was sold several times before she finally sprang a leak in January 1935 and was abandoned off Newfoundland. Her crew drifted for two days before they arrived at the French island of St. Pierre, off southeastern Newfoundland.

The Bluenose went on to beat other Gloucestermen, sailing away from ten other Nova Scotia schooners who challenged her. In 1942, her racing days far behind her, the Bluenose was fitted with diesel engines and sold to the West Indies Trading Company. She plied the islands, laden with bananas and rum, but in late January 1946, her back broken by a storm, she sank on a coral reef off Haiti. Today, her image is perpetuated on the Canadian dime and in the lines of the Bluenose II, a schooner patterned after the original but packed with modern amenities never known to the old saltbanker.

Percy Williams

RELUCTANT RUNNER
BY BRUCE LEVETT
THE CANADIAN PRESS, TORONTO

A skinny youngster came out of Vancouver to beat the best in the world in the 100-metre dash. And while his town and his country were howling in glee over this accomplishment, he took the whole thing one step further and won the 200-metre run as well. Can you imagine it happening today? What sort of a hero would this guy be? One thing is for sure, he would be set up for life with money from endorsements. Ah, but this was 1928 and the place was Amsterdam and this was, after all, amateur athletics in its purest form.

Four year later, Percy Williams went to another Olympics in Los Angeles as the reigning Olympic champion in the 100 and the 200. He went there as captain of the Canadian team, and he was handed a one-way ticket and a ten dollar bill to cover expenses. Williams was not particularly surprised. That was the way things were back in 1932—and, indeed, the way things were until relatively recently.

The Olympic Games were not—no matter what you may have been led to believe—for the athletes. Not back in the old days. They were for the self-important officials called ''the badgers'' — the people who made the rules. They were known as ''the badgers'' because their main aim in life was to collect Olympic lapel badges from as many other countries as possible. However, this story is not about the badgers. This story is about Percy Williams and one other guy — Bob Granger. He didn't like the badgers any more than Percy did. And, in the end, they both beat them.

Want to go all the way back? OK — Percy made his mark first at the age of thirteen, in 1921, when he came second in a 100-yard dash. That was it for a while because, two years later, he fell ill with rheumatic fever and doctors told him his heart was damaged. No more strenuous exercise, they said.

Percy took it easy until he reached the age of eighteen, and then he accepted a challenge to run against the city champion in his home town of Vancouver. They finished in a dead heat. By the following year, 1926, he was running in the city championships and he set a city record that stood for more than forty years. The British Columbia championships followed, then the Canadian, and then —a year later—the Canadian Olympic trials.

Somewhere in there, Granger appeared on the scene, a man ten years older than Williams and a freelance coach of swimmers, rugger players and runners. It was a strange pairing. Williams begrudged the effort required to become a world champion while Granger, on the other hand, was a fanatic—but a fanatic with the soul of a poet. He lied to the kid and he goaded him — anything to make happen what he was convinced had to happen.

Percy Williams really didn't want to run. In later years he insisted that patriotism — running for flag and country—was a crock. So why did he do it? ''You kind of got pushed into these things,'' he said later in life. ''You had to help the school. You were a bum if you didn't try out.''

Granger built on that. He was also convinced that ''the kid ran best on hate,'' so he set about to build up a little hate. At one point, he forged a letter, signing it with the name of a prominent competitor, in which he wrote that Williams didn't have a chance in a forthcoming meet. ''After stewing all night on his adrenalin, Williams licked the field,'' Granger recalled years later.

If anything, the badgers had even less regard for Granger than they did for the athletes. He wasn't a real coach, they said. And when it came time for the 1928 Olympic Games in Amsterdam, there was no place on the team for him. He got there anyway, but it wasn't easy. Granger worked his way across Canada in the dining car of a train as a pantry boy, and across the Atlantic as part of the crew of a freighter. Any expense money he had was raised by Williams's mother. But he did get there. In Amsterdam, he worked on Williams's starts by placing a mattress against a wall and powering his runner into it. At night, to make certain his boy was not disturbed, Granger slept on the floor outside Williams's door.

In later life, Williams gave full credit to Granger for his Olympic gold, despite his impatience with Granger's training methods. And those methods were unusual. Ever mindful of the doctors' warning that Williams should avoid strenuous exercise, Granger took great care of his athlete. He gave him cocoa-butter rubdowns and massages. Before each meet he dressed Williams in three track suits, four sweaters and blankets, so his boy would be warmed and ready each time he went to the post.

In Amsterdam, when Williams beat the gods of the running world, Jack London, George Lammers, Frank Wykoff, Wilfred Legg and Bob McAllister in the 100, Granger wept. When Williams passed Jacob Schuller, Jackson Scholz, Walter Rangeley and Helmut Koernig in the 200 for his second gold, Granger gripped a barbed-wire fence in excitement and greeted his protegé with hands covered in blood.

Charlie Paddock, coach of the United States sprint team, said Williams was the only sprinter he ever saw who could employ two running styles in a single race. "He commences the race as a pull runner (leg action in front of him, knees coming up). In the closing metres, he is not a pull runner at all, but distinctly a driver."

The *chef de mission* for the U.S. team, General Douglas MacArthur, watched the kid from Vancouver annihilate his aces and shook his head. "He is the greatest sprinter the world has ever seen," MacArthur told reporters.

Was this an upset? Believe it. The Canadian's victory in the 100 was so unexpected that the medal presentations had to be postponed while flunkies thrashed about in search of a Canadian flag. But if this was unexpected insofar as the track world was concerned, how did it affect the new champion? He wrote in his diary, under the date of July 30, 1928: "So I'm supposed to be the world's 100-metre champion. Crushed apples. No more fun in running now."

No new worlds to conquer? Well — maybe one more. The following day, Williams went out and became the world's 200-metre champion as well. He is the only Canadian ever to win the incredible sprint double. Still — he had a point. Where *do* you go from there? Williams went home. He tried to go to university, but it was no good. Come and run for us, they pleaded. Come and speak at our banquet. Williams went back to the track.

In later years, he would maintain that winning the sprint double was not the finest feat of his career. "I think I came up with my best performance a few months later, in the winter of 1929," he said. "I went east and ran the indoor circuit. I had never run indoors before, but I ran 22 races in 21 days. I came second in one of them and won all the others. Everyone remembers Amsterdam, but nobody remembers that."

In Toronto, on August 9, 1930, he ran the 100 metres in 10.3 seconds, a world record that stood for eleven years. A few days later, warmed and readied by Granger as always, Williams lined up in the 100-yard dash in Hamilton at the first running of what was then known as the British Empire Games. There was a delay and the fragile Williams cooled out. He was 65 yards down the track when something tore in his left thigh. He hit the tape first, then crumbled.

That was it, although he tried a comeback for the 1932 Olympics in Los Angeles. That was it, also, for Bob Granger. Oh, there was one more Olympics with one more athlete for the coach, but there were no more medals.

Williams and Granger—both life-long bachelors—faded from the track scene. Williams spent a hitch in the RCAF as a pilot instructor, and then, for the rest of a lonely life, sold insurance. Granger? He fell from sight for many years, then was discovered living on his old-age pension in a room over a barber shop in Alberni, British Columbia. He had no pictures, no mementoes, no clippings to mark an incredible time.

But he did have memories. A young reporter named Dennis Orchard found him and listened to his reminiscences. ''Lots of people knew the ordinary good Williams,'' Granger said. ''Only I knew the extraordinary good Williams.'' No sprinter since, he said, ''matched that half-driving, half-skimming artistry of style.''

When Williams set his 100-metre mark of 10.3 seconds against a stiff wind, in Toronto, ''I wanted to feast my eyes on the sight,'' Granger said. ''I wanted the finish line to run before him to the ends of the earth. He was thistledown before the summer breeze.''

Left: Percy Williams

Preceding page: Williams breaks the tape

Shore and Bailey

BY MEL SUFRIN
THE CANADIAN PRESS, TORONTO

Old-time hockey fans remember Eddie Shore as the most talented defenceman of his era, celebrated for his end-to-end rushes and devastating body checks in the 1920s and '30s when he starred for the Boston Bruins. Unfortunately, Shore's brilliant career was marred by a single incident of violence that still ranks as the most dramatic in the history of the National Hockey League.

It occurred on December 12, 1933, in Boston Garden in a regular-season game with the Toronto Maple Leafs. With Toronto playing two men short, Shore, after being body-checked into the boards by Red Horner, was skating out of the Leafs' end. Ace Bailey was facing the other way when Shore, apparently mistaking him for Horner, knocked his feet out from under him. When Bailey's head hit the ice and he went into convulsions, Horner retaliated

by knocking Shore out with a single punch, administering a cut that required seven stitches.

Because a blood clot had formed between Bailey's skull and brain, doctors had to drill a hole into the side of his head in a three-hour operation to get at the clot. The Toronto left-winger was unconscious and near death for fifteen days and, as daily bulletins were being issued, Canadians were asked to pray for his recovery. He was released from hospital after five weeks but never played hockey again, although he spent many years as an employee of Maple Leaf Gardens.

Shore was suspended for sixteen games but spent part of the time in hospital recovering from his injuries. Horner was suspended for six games.

When Shore died in hospital in Springfield, Massachusetts on March 16, 1985, at the age of eighty-two,

Bailey was interviewed in Toronto. He said he felt no bitterness. "It was something that could have happened to anyone." And Bailey knew that Shore deeply regretted the affair.

Shore, a native of Fort Qu'Appelle, Saskatchewan, led the Bruins to two Stanley Cups, in 1929 and 1939. He scored 108 goals and assisted on 179, a remarkable figure for the days when defencemen were primarily assigned to guarding the blue line. Shore also remains the only defenceman to have won the Hart Trophy as most valuable player four times, a feat accomplished first in the 1932–33 season and finally in 1937–38. A notable exception was the 1933–34 season, the one in which the Ace Bailey incident occurred.

Shore shakes Bailey's hand

The Big Upset—1936

BY NEIL STEVENS
THE CANADIAN PRESS, TORONTO

During the past twenty-five years, Canadians have had an elusive dream —to win the Olympic and world ice hockey championships. But there once was a time when Canada could rely on its amateur champions to bring gold home every time.

Canada won the first four Olympic hockey tournaments, in 1920, 1924, 1928 and 1932, without a single defeat. In 1936, when the Canadian all-star squad arrived in Garmisch-Partenkirchen, West Germany, as the favorites, it was taken for granted that, once again, they would display their superiority on the ice to the whole world. What followed—a 2–1 loss to England— was a shocker, as Canada suffered its first Olympic hockey defeat on Tuesday, February 11, 1936.

The groundwork for the upset had been laid years before by one of the English team managers, John Francis (Bunny) Ahearne, who later became president of the International Ice Hockey Federation (IIHF), and who, until his retirement in 1975, stubbornly refused to allow Canada to use professionals in world championship tournaments. In the early 1930s, Ahearne had obtained lists of players affiliated with the Canadian Amateur Hockey Association (CAHA), and began recruiting British-born players for a new British hockey league.

When England's 1936 Olympic team took to the ice, it turned out, therefore, that all but one of the players were Canadian-trained. Before the tournament began, Canada protested that goaltender Jimmy Foster and forward Alex Archer had not obtained proper transfer papers from the CAHA. The IIHF upheld the protest but Canada subsequently waived its objection, figuring the English hockey federation would withdraw Foster and Archer to ensure CAHA co-operation on future transfers.

But the Canadian-trained members of the English team remained in the lineup and were vital in their team's monumental victory. Other Canadian-trained players in the English lineup included Archie Stinchcombe of Windsor, Ontario, and Jim Chappel of Whitby, Ontario. Although Canada controlled the tempo of the game, the English capitalized on their few scoring chances and received standout goaltending from Foster, who had backstopped the Moncton Hawks to the Allan Cup title in 1933 and 1934.

Canada was shocked when John Davey of Port Arthur, Ontario, scored England's first goal after only twenty seconds, by lofting a floater from the Canadian blue line that was missed by goaltender Frank (Dinty) Moore of the Port Colborne (Ontario) Sailors.

Ralph St. Germain of the Montreal Royals tied it for Canada 1–1 later in the first period and, after a scoreless middle period, with six minutes remaining, the English won it on a goal made by Ed Brenchley of Niagara Falls, Ontario.

A complicated tournament format provided for three phases of competition, with only the second and third phases counting in the final standings. Canada had sailed through the first round with three consecutive victories. The loss to England came in Canada's opening second-round game. Canada then won its final two second-round games and both its medal-round games against the United States and Czechoslovakia.

But Canada did not get another shot at England. Because the two countries advanced out of the same pool, they, therefore, did not meet in the final round. One report from Germany said the Canadian team had threatened to withdraw unless it was given a chance to play England again in the medal round, but Canadian team officials denied the report.

With German leader Adolf Hitler in the stands and the sun beating down on a slushy ice surface, Canada completed its tournament schedule with a 1–0 win over the United States. Because England and the United States had fought to a scoreless draw the previous day, Canada's final-day victory over the Americans ensured England the championship and the gold medal. Canada was forced to settle for silver. On Monday, February 17, 1936, a bold headline on the front page of a Toronto

Left: J.F. (Bunny) Ahearne
Right: The Gold Medal Team

newspaper broke the mournful news to Canadians: ''England Wins Olympic Hockey Title.''

''While we lost the title, we know we have the best club,'' said Canadian coach Albert Pudas of Port Arthur. ''The boys and I have only one regret—that we had to be the first to let Canada down.''

But right from the start, there had been controversy about the Canadian team entry. The original Canadian lineup had included four members of the Halifax Wolverines, who had won the Allan Cup in 1935. When the Wolverines disbanded, an all-star team was formed for the Olympics.

However, just before the team was to sail to Europe, the four Halifax players were dropped when it was alleged they had asked for financial aid to keep their families afloat while they were off representing their country. In one of its final exhibitions on the East Coast before departing for the games, the Olympic team was pelted with bottles by Maritimers upset that their local heroes had been bushwacked by the bureaucrats.

With Foster and the other Canadian-trained players forming the backbone of the English club, the killing stroke took place and the

Canadians lost, never again to regain their pre-eminence in the Olympic and world ice hockey championships.

INSET: Jim Kelly

GREAT BRITAIN
Olympic Champions—1936

Standing—left to right: J. F. AHEARNE (Secretary, B.I.H.A.) and Team Manager, J. CHAPPELL   A. STINCHCOMBE   A. ARCHER

G. DAILLEY   P. NICKLIN (Coach)   J. KILPATRICK   J. FOSTER   J. COWARD   G. DAVEY   P. V. HUNTER (Pres. B.I.H.A.)

Kneeling—left to right: R. WYMAN   J. BORLAND   A. CHILD   E. BRENCHLEY

Not included is C. ERHARDT (Team Captain)

The Longest Game

THE MONTREAL MARATHON
BY DAVID GERSOVITZ
THE CANADIAN PRESS, MONTREAL

The Great Depression was the era of marathons. People, in search of fame and a few square meals, danced until they dropped, and six-day bike races were all the rage. The National Hockey League had marathons, too, and none more memorable than the one on March 24–25, 1936, when the Montreal Maroons and the Detroit Red Wings locked horns in a Stanley Cup semifinal for 176 minutes 30 seconds.

The game, the opener of a best-of-five series, started at 8:34 p.m. and ended at 2:25 a.m. when Detroit rookie Modere (Mud) Bruneteau picked up a rolling puck left by teammate Hec Kilrea and swatted it past Montreal goalie Lorne Chabot at 16:30 of the sixth overtime period. It was the only goal of the longest game in NHL history. That endurance contest beat the previous record set in 1933, when the Boston Bruins and the Toronto Maple Leafs had battled in a playoff game for 162 minutes 40 seconds.

Bruneteau's game-winning goal was the classic instance of the right player in the right place at the right time. The goal, however, brought a moment of stunned silence from the 9,000 Montreal Forum fans, followed by a loud cheer—an outpouring of relief. Most of the fans had stayed to the end and, as Tuesday gave way to Wednesday, anxious relatives called The Forum about fans long overdue at home. "They're stealing my stuff," wisecracked six-day biker Bill Spencer as the game lurched past midnight.

Referees Ag Smith and Bill Stewart skated the whole 176 minutes. They couldn't remove their skates between overtime periods for fear their feet would swell up and they would never get the boots back on. Broadcasters Charlie Harwood, with the English play-by-play, and Roland Beaudry, with the French, also worked non-stop.

The game itself started at a fast clip, but became increasingly cautious as both teams feared a fatal error. As the overtime progressed and the players neared collapse, play became even more timid with only an occasional organized rush.

Between overtime periods, the Maroons sipped coffee and the Red Wings tea, "both beverages," as one newspaper wag observed, "being slightly reinforced to keep their pepper up during the marathon." It was later asserted that the 30 players had lost an average of five pounds each.

The heroes, aside from Bruneteau, were goaltenders Chabot and Norm Smith. Smith, a Maroons castoff, turned back 90 Montreal shots in his first NHL playoff game, while Chabot stopped all but one of 67 Detroit shots.

One Montreal reporter called Smith lucky, "sensationally so at times," but conceded he made several big saves. The Maroons held a territorial advantage throughout the game and remained confident afterwards that they would rebound. "Smith was good, but he was lucky, too," said Montreal manager Tommy Gorman. "We'll take the Wings, and once Smith cracks, it will be all over."

But Smith, one of the last goalies in the league to sport a cap on the ice, never did crack. He didn't yield a goal until the thirteenth minute of the third game, when Gus Marker tallied for the Maroons. It was the only goal Smith surrendered in the Wings' three-game sweep of Montreal, and his shutout streak of 248 minutes 32 seconds is an NHL playoff record.

Detroit went on to whip the Toronto Maple Leafs in the best-of-five Stanley Cup final 3–1.

Mud Bruneteau

Lorne Chabot

Gerard Côté

HEARTBREAK HILL
BY JOHN MACKINNON
THE CANADIAN PRESS, MONTREAL

For a lot of runners, Boston's Heartbreak Hill is a place they think about with dread, but four-time Boston Marathon winner Gerard Côté recalls the last hill on the storied course with fondness. Four times in an eight-year span during the 1940s, Côté's stamina and smooth stride carried him past his rivals at or near that 90-foot rise at mile 21 of the Boston route. He posted victories in 1940, '43, '44 and '48.

"That's mostly the race there," Côté recalled of the series of four hills that undulate between miles 18 and 21, culminating in the final test of Heartbreak Hill. "If it doesn't break your heart, it will break your legs. But if you're solid there, you're going to be hard to beat."

On April 19, 1940, Côté had no doubt he'd be in good shape at Heartbreak Hill, which coincides with the point of a marathon when many competitors are straining against what runners call "The Wall," the period when the muscles are energy-drained and exhaustion sets in. Côté had been training 120 miles a week and, for several weeks before the race, had intensified his workouts on a brutal course

in Central Falls, Rhode Island. Côté ran this course, which featured a hill per mile, wearing a track suit and heavy running shoes. "I was really trained for more than 26 miles," he said. "That's why, after 19 miles on the day of the race, my strength was just coming out."

During that 1940 marathon, U.S. runner Johnny Kelley crested Heartbreak Hill in the lead with Rob Rankin of Toronto second and Côté a well-placed third. The two front-

runners exchanged the lead briefly on the downslope while Côté prepared to make his move. He overtook the spent Rankin, then powered past Kelley at the intersection of Beacon Street and Dean Road. "At 23 miles, Tom Kennedy (a race official) told me, 'You're running about 12 miles an hour,' " said Côté. "I told him, 'Let's go for 13.' "

Côté's pace was the fastest it had been in the race when he broke across the finish line in two hours 28 minutes 28.6 seconds, a course record. Kelley was second, nearly four minutes behind the Ste-Barnabé, Quebec, native. Rankin finished eighth. "The last five or six miles is one big yell, one big standing ovation," said Côté. "That makes you nervous and it makes you run. I was good for at least ten more miles at the end of the race.

Côté also won the 1940 Yonkers Marathon, recognized then as the American Athletic Union championship race, and was named winner of the Lou Marsh Trophy, presented to Canada's athlete of the year. In 1943 and again in 1944, he would outrace Kelley to win at Boston. And in 1948, he outduelled another U.S. runner, Ted Vogel, to win a record fourth Boston race.

That record stood until 1980, forty years after Côté's first victory, when hometown hero Bill Rodgers won his third straight and fourth overall Boston Marathon.

1942 Stanley Cup

BY IAN MACLAINE
THE CANADIAN PRESS, TORONTO

It was billed at the time as one of the most memorable events in Canadian sport. And more than forty years later, the memory of the 1941–42 Stanley Cup final between the Toronto Maple Leafs and the Detroit Red Wings remains untarnished.

The Leafs, second-place finishers at the end of the 48-game National Hockey League season and down three games to a team that had finished fifth in the standings, were to make an incredible recovery in an era scarred by the Second World War. Neither before nor since has a team battled back from a three-game deficit to win a best-of-seven final.

Pete Langelle, an unlikely hero, and goaltender Turk Broda etched their names in the hearts of Toronto fans forever in that series. Langelle capped the Leaf resurgence with the winning goal in the second period of a 3–1 victory in the seventh game, while Broda's acrobatic netminding made the comeback possible.

Toronto manager Conn Smythe, who had fought all odds almost single-handedly to build Toronto's Maple Leaf Gardens a decade earlier along with the franchise, had not yet left to lead troops into battle in Europe.

But the Germans would have been friendlier than some Toronto supporters when Smythe responded to the first three losses by benching Gordie Drillon—the only Leaf ever to win a scoring title and the team's high scorer in four of the previous five years—and inserting untested rookie Don Metz on a line with his brother Nick and Dave (Sweeney) Shriner.

Jack Adams was at his combative best in those years as manager-coach of a powerful Detroit organization.

Many NHL stars of that era, some of whom would eventually enlist in Canada's armed forces, dotted the lineups of both teams—Broda, Syl Apps, Shriner, Bucko McDonald, Bob Goldham, Billy Taylor and the Metz brothers with the Leafs; Black Jack Stewart, Jimmy Orlando, Don Grosso, Mud Bruneteau, Sid Abel and Joe Carveth in Detroit livery.

Grosso scored two game winners

as Detroit shocked the Toronto crowds, 3–2 and 4–2, in the first two games at the Gardens. And the Red Wings looked set to nail the coffin shut on the Leafs by winning the third game in Detroit 5–2.

That setback sparked the indomitable Smythe to take drastic measures. It was the Major who coined the adage, "If you can't beat 'em in the alley, you can't beat them on the ice." Every Leaf was made aware of his philosophy.

Drillon had a magical touch around the net and rarely drew a penalty, an attribute that did not win him high marks in the Smythe school of hockey ethics. More to the point, he tended to leave defensive chores to his linemates. So Smythe, imper-

vious to the howls of Drillon supporters, benched his high-scoring right winger, who never played for the Leafs again. And the line of the Metz brothers and Shriner played a significant role in the series. Nick Metz's goal late in the fourth game at Detroit's Olympia salvaged a 4–3 Toronto win and seemingly prolonged the inevitable.

When the teams returned to the Gardens, Shriner and Don Metz did a number on the Wings, Shriner with four goals and Metz with three and two assists, as the Leafs romped over Detroit 9–3.

Broda was at his spectacular best when the teams returned to Detroit as Don Metz broke a scoreless tie in the second period and Shriner col-

lected two assists in a 3–0 victory that evened the series at three games each.

The portly Broda, an inconsistent regular-season performer, was once labelled by a Toronto writer as the ancient mariner who stoppeth one of three. But throughout his lengthy career he always seemed to rise above himself at playoff time. The Turk was the deciding factor again in the seventh game. Veteran Leaf fans still insist that he was the greatest money goaltender of all time.

Left: The Leafs score
Centre: Turk Broda
Right: Syl Apps with the Stanley Cup

Dick Fowler

STARTING OVER

BY MIKE RUTSEY
THE CANADIAN PRESS, TORONTO

In the waning days of the 1945 baseball season, Dick Fowler was gripped by nervous excitement as he stepped on the mound at historic Shibe Park in Philadelphia to start the second game of an American League doubleheader for Connie Mack's Athletics. He felt like the rawest of rookies and with good reason. Although the strapping six-foot-four, 215 pound right-hander had started 30 other major league games since moving up from the Toronto Maple Leafs of the International League in 1941, this was his first start in close to three years. Fowler, a product of the Toronto sandlots, had been taking part in a far bigger game where he wore the khaki uniform of the Canadian Army. Discharged just twenty-four days earlier, he had only two relief appearances under his belt prior to being tabbed to start the second game on September 9 against the St. Louis Browns.

The crowd was in good spirits that Sunday afternoon as the woeful Athletics had topped the Browns, the American League champions the previous season, 6–2 in the opener. The second game was scoreless as Fowler carried a no-hitter into the ninth inning against a rookie pitcher named George Miller, who came close to matching his brilliance. Fowler got a scare in the ninth when he walked Mike Byrnes, one of four bases on balls he issued, and Lou Finney almost ended his no-hitter and shut-out with one swing when he drilled a shot down the right-field

Below: Fowler with 'Cheif' Bender (left), and Connie Mack (centre)

line that just hooked foul. The young pitcher bore down, however, and induced Finney to ground into an inning-ending double play.

Hal Peck quickly made sure Fowler's superb effort didn't go to waste as he tripled home Irving Hall to give the Athletics a 1–0 victory and his pitcher a spot in the record books. ''My curve and my changeup were working perfectly,'' Fowler said. ''I'm certainly glad this came against the Browns. They beat me 1–0 in a 16-inning game here in 1942.''

Because the surrender of Japan and the end of the Second World War were dominating the news, back in Toronto Fowler's heroics received scant coverage, and *The Telegram* and *The Star* ran only brief stories of his feat.

Fowler, who died in 1972, went on to win 66 games over parts of nine seasons, but none would come close to equalling the excitement of that first time back on the mound. On August 7, 1985, Dick Fowler was inducted into the Canadian Baseball Hall of Fame.

Jackie Robinson

BREAKTHROUGH
BY WESLEY GOLDSTEIN
THE CANADIAN PRESS, MONTREAL

When the Montreal Royals brought the first black player into organized baseball, it was considered a questionable experiment. However, within the short space of a year, the all-white establishment world had to acknowledge the success of the move.

The drama began on October 23, 1945, in Delormier Stadium, where the late Branch Rickey Jr. introduced a quiet, twenty-six-year-old infielder named Jackie Robinson as his newest acquisition for the Royals. It ended one year later in the same place as Montreal, the top farm team of the Brooklyn Dodgers, defeated the Louisville Colonels in six games to capture the Little World Series.

"My selfish objective is to win ball games," Rickey, Brooklyn's minor-league director, said at that October 23rd press conference. "I never

meant to be a crusader, and I hope I won't be regarded as one." No matter how Rickey had been regarded at the outset, by the completion of the 1946 season he looked like a genius. It wasn't easy, though, not for Rickey, not for the Royals, and especially not for Robinson.

After he and the team struggled through a tormented spring in Florida, Robinson gave a demonstration of things to come, stroking four hits, including a home run, in five at-bats on opening day. The new Montreal second baseman scored four times, drove in three runs and stole two bases as the visiting Royals drubbed Jersey City 14–1.

Over the season, Robinson led the International League with a .349 batting average and 113 runs scored.

Montreal won 100 games, lost 54, and ran away with their second con-

secutive league pennant, taking the flag by 19 and a half games. Although Robinson was certainly an integral part of Montreal's success, the 1946 Royals were also blessed with a well-balanced, talent-laden roster that included former and future major leaguers Marvin Rackley, Tom Tatum, Al Campanis, Red Durrett, Earl Naylor and John (Spider) Jorgensen.

When the final out was recorded against the Colonels in the Little World Series, the appreciative fans streamed into the streets outside of Delormier in search of the one man who made the Montreal Royals baseball's most talked about team in 1946. Robinson had to be "rescued" from the crowd by a passing motorist, an event that prompted a black American reporter to write: "It was probably the only day in history that a black man ran from a white mob with love, instead of lynching, on its mind."

Below: Robinson slides safely into third in his first game with Montreal

Barbara Ann Scott

THE GIRL WHO CHANGED FIGURE SKATING FOREVER

BY GRAHAM COX
THE CANADIAN PRESS, OTTAWA

There was no one like her before 1947 and there has been no one like Barbara Ann Scott since. It seems improbable that this petite, blonde eighteen-year-old figure skater could, in only two brief years, create such an impact on Canadian sports and so captivate fans around the world. And, almost unnoticed, she changed the face of women's figure skating while she did it.

From the time Scott started skating at age seven at the Minto Skating Club in Ottawa, it seemed almost ordained that she would win the women's world championship in 1947 and 1948 and the Olympic gold medal in 1948 at St. Moritz, Switzerland. By 1940 she was already Canada's national junior champion, moving on to hold the national senior title from 1944 through 1948.

When the five-foot-two, 100 pound whirlwind finished her four-minute free skate at the 1947 World Championships in Stockholm with three double loop jumps in succession, the perfect 6.0 marks awarded by two of the judges seemed merely a necessary confirmation of the roars of approval from 15,000 fans.

Scott's homecoming after that 1947 victory as the first North American world champion, man or woman, was described by police as "surpassing everything, including royal visits." She was fêted and adored for her victory, but the best was still to come. That was at St. Moritz where she not only defended her title, but added the Olympic crown, again a first for a North American skater.

The one cloud to darken that perfect year was a ruling by Avery Brundage, chairman of the Interna-

tional Olympic committee, that Scott could not accept the canary yellow convertible her adoring Ottawa fans wanted to give her. He said she would have to return her Olympic medal if she accepted the car, which then sat unused for years in a warehouse waiting for an owner.

Years later, Scott made light of the adulation she received before spending five years as a professional with the Hollywood Ice Review. "You know, it was after the war and people were looking for something to cheer about," she said on a visit

to Toronto from her Chicago home where she has lived with her husband, Thomas V. King, since 1955.

What Scott didn't mention were the changes she forced on women's figure skating with her performances. Until then, women had basically glided and swooped gracefully about the ice in the manner of Sonja Henie, the Norwegian doll credited with making the sport popular. But the athletic style Scott took to the 1947 championships, and the close of her 1948 performance with three double salchow jumps, forev-

er changed the face of women's skating.

Scott's coach, Sheldon Galbraith, said of her: "Barbara Ann was a brilliant girl to work with. I had never experienced anything of that magnitude before." And international skating judge Ralph McCreath of Toronto said of her 1947 championship: "Barbara Ann is executing spins, turns and jumps so far advanced they were unheard of ten years ago—even by men skaters."

Named Canada's outstanding athlete in 1945, 1947 and 1948, and eventually made a member of the Canadian Sports Hall of Fame, Barbara Ann Scott turned to breeding and showing horses where, to no one's surprise, she has once again attained an international reputation.

Gordie Howe

MR. HOCKEY
BY NEIL STEVENS
THE CANADIAN PRESS, TORONTO

On March 28, 1950, Gordie Howe was carried off the ice of the Detroit Olympia on a stretcher. He was bleeding profusely from a bad gash under his right eye, his nose was shattered and his skull was fractured. The next day, two days short of his twenty-second birthday, Howe underwent brain surgery. The Detroit Red Wings' right winger had taken a run at Toronto centre Teeder Kennedy late in the first game of a Stanley Cup semifinal, missed the Maple Leaf captain and crashed head first into the boards near his team's bench.

For twenty-four hours Howe's life was in doubt. He spent two weeks in hospital, and it was feared his promising hockey career would be cut tragically short. Thirty years later, at age fifty-two, Howe was still playing in the National Hockey League. Not only did Howe recover and play longer in the NHL than any other player before or since, he established a myriad of records which still stand, including most goals (801), most assists (1,049) and most points (1,850). Howe's exploits earned him the nickname "Mr. Hockey" from writers around the NHL.

His legendary career came about because of an incident in Saskatoon, Saskatchewan, in 1933 when Howe was five. A destitute woman appeared at the family's front door asking for a dollar so she could buy milk for her children. She insisted Catherine Howe take a bag of odds and ends in return, and a pair of skates was included in the offering. The skates were too big for the little boy but rags were stuffed into the toes to make them fit.

Eleven years later, Howe was signed by the Red Wings. The New York Rangers had given him a tryout but turned him down. After a year of minor-professional hockey in Omaha, Nebraska, he stepped into the NHL with Detroit in 1946 at age eighteen. Howe scored only seven goals in his first season but kept improving. It was while playing on a line with Ted Lindsay and Sid Abel —The Production Line—that the six-foot, 200-pounder made his mark.

The Red Wings won the Stanley Cup while Howe recuperated from his terrible head injury in the spring of 1950. Defying the doctors, he returned the next season to win the first of six scoring championships. In 1951–52, Howe won the scoring title again and was named the NHL's most valuable player. The season was capped by another Stanley Cup

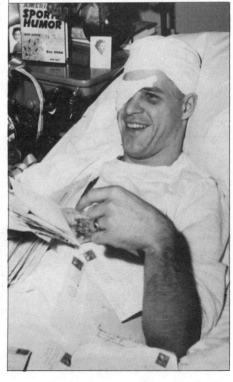

Left: Barbara Ann Scott practising for 1948 Olympics

Right: Howe recovering in a Detroit hospital, April 4, 1950

triumph. The Red Wings would win the Cup again in 1953–54 and 1954–55 and Howe would go on to take the Hart Memorial Trophy as the league's most valuable player another five times.

The awards were not solely a tribute to his scoring. Watchers of Howe in his prime recall games in which it seemed as if his number 9 jersey was being worn by two players at once. Leading a rush on the net, he would reappear at the

other end within seconds to thwart an apparent breakaway by the opposition. Later, when he could no longer keep up with younger skaters, he would slow the game down to his own pace. Shifting a defenceman out of position, he would poke the puck between the defender's legs and continue toward the net or slide a deft pass to an uncovered teammate. Howe's strength and toughness equalled his shooting and skating ability; few opponents chose to fight

him as his punishing elbows were as much a part of his reputation as his goals.

In 1971, Howe, bothered by an arthritic left wrist, retired and the Detroit club gave him a front-office job. But it didn't suit ''The Big Guy,'' as teammates had nicknamed him, and he became bored and quit.

Below: Howe scores against Johnny Bower

Right: Gordie Howe scores his 545th goal to become the all-time goal-scoring leader

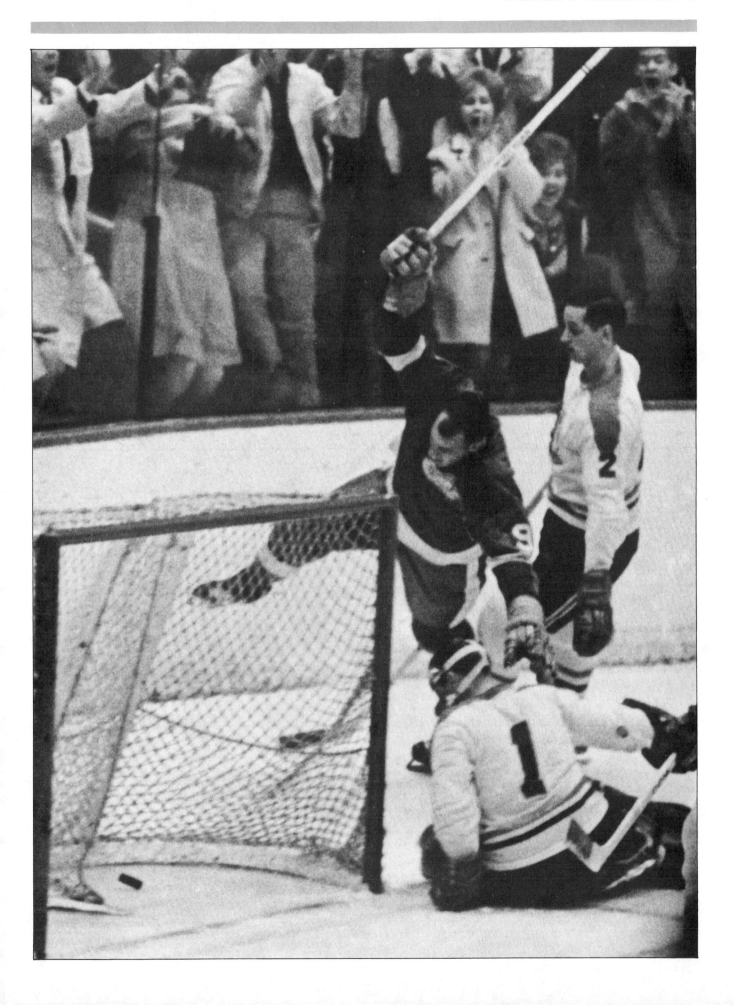

He was elected to the Hockey Hall of Fame in 1972. But instead of fading away, he accepted a $1-million offer in 1973 from the new World Hockey Association and the opportunity to play on the same team as his sons Mark and Marty. The Howes moved to Houston to play for the Aeros. Gordie, Mark and Marty were together for four years in Houston and moved over to the New England Whalers in 1977. They had one final year together after the Whalers joined the NHL in 1979 before Gordie finally called it quits after playing professional hockey for thirty-three years.

"During five decades, Gordie Howe was synonymous with outstanding and almost unbelievable athletic achievement," NHL president John Ziegler said at the time. "An assembly of everything that was ever written about him would still be insufficient to describe his achievements and contributions."

Today, Howe is a special assistant to Howard Baldwin, chairman of the Hartford Whalers. He continues to tour NHL rinks, drawing crowds, signing autographs and chatting with fans. He still laces on his skates for charity functions. In September 1984, in a game in Toronto between members of the 1972 NHL Summit Series team and a band of all-star oldtimers, Howe scored the winning goal for the all-stars. He was fifty-six at the time.

Below: Howe's famous elbows in action, 1978

Right: Roger Bannister crosses the finish line ahead of John Landy

Miracle Mile

BY GRANT KERR
THE CANADIAN PRESS, VANCOUVER

Long before the opening parade of athletes at the 1954 British Empire Games, the meeting of milers Roger Bannister of England and John Landy of Australia had been labelled as the premier event of the quadrennial sports festival.

The middle-distance event at Empire Stadium in Vancouver more than lived up to its billing on August 7 when Bannister and Landy became the first men to run the mile in less than four minutes in the same race. Landy held the world record at three minutes 57.9 seconds; Bannister had been the first man to break the four-minute barrier three months earlier.

In this truly classic race, Bannister won the gold medal in 3:58.8 and Landy the silver in 3:59.9.

Bannister did his final training race on the lush grounds of a golf course at the University of British Columbia. He had a cold in his chest and worried about his attitude as race time grew near. "I am certain that one's feelings at the last minute before a race matter most," Bannister later wrote. "Confidence that has been supreme until the final moment can be lost quite suddenly."

There were eight finalists in the mile, including Rich Ferguson of Vancouver, who would win the

bronze medal in 4:04.6. But this day belonged to Bannister and Landy, and Landy was the pre-race favorite.

Bill Baillie of New Zealand took the early lead in the race and Bannister stayed back in third place, behind Landy. The Australian took over the lead and completed the first lap seven yards ahead of Bannister. Landy stayed ahead at the half and three-quarter marks and Bannister recalls thinking the Australian was going to break the world record again.

Quickening his stride, Bannister was at Landy's shoulder like a shadow, his strides becoming more painful with the quick tempo. "It was incredible that in a race at this speed he should start a finishing burst 300 yards from the tape," Bannister said. "If Landy did not slacken soon, I would be finished." Bannister tried

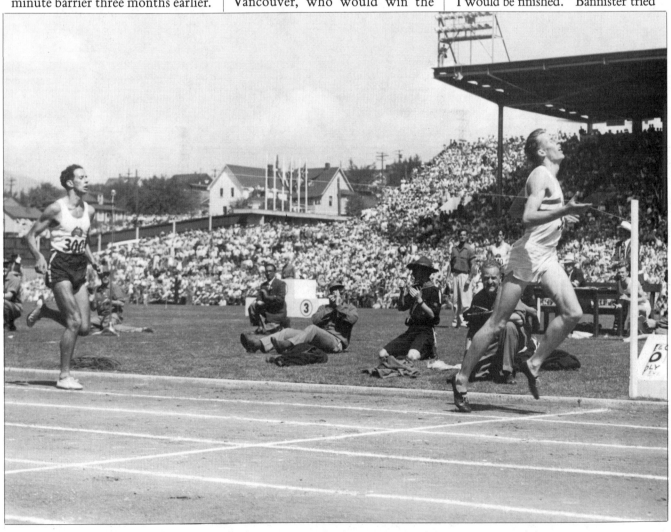

to convince himself that Landy was tiring, and decided that, if he was to pass Landy, it would have to be on the final bend.

In a moment now commemorated by a bronzed statue in front of Empire Stadium, Bannister and Landy made racing history. "Just before the end of the last bend, I flung myself past Landy," Bannister recalled. "As I did so, I saw him glance inwards over his opposite shoulder. This tiny act of his held great significance. The moment he looked around he was unprotected against me and so lost a valuable fraction of a second in his response to my challenge. It was my tremendous luck that these two happenings — his turning around and my final spurt — came absolutely simultaneously."

Bannister took the lead with 70 yards remaining and managed to hold it to the tape in what was truly called the "Miracle Mile". Praising Landy lavishly, the Englishman called the last lap the most exciting and intense moments of his life. "Landy had shown me what a race could really be at its greatest," added Bannister. "His boldness forced me to abandon my time schedule and lose myself quite completely in the struggle itself. After this experience I felt that I could never be interested again in record-breaking without the thrill of competitive struggle."

Below: Roger Bannister near collapse after the Miracle Mile
Right: Marilyn Bell strikes out across Lake Ontario

Marilyn Bell

THE UNDERDOG CHAMPION

BY DAVID JENSEN
THE CANADIAN PRESS, TORONTO

There's just no telling what can happen when a Canadian feels slighted. Take the case of Marilyn Bell, the Canadian schoolgirl who was the first person to swim the 32 miles across Lake Ontario from Youngstown, New York, to Toronto.

When Marilyn heard that American marathon champion, Florence Chadwick, and three other swimmers planned to attempt the long distance swim, she wondered why Canadians had been excluded from the challenge. Chadwick, thirty-four, and famous for swimming across the English Channel, had been offered $2,500 by the Canadian National Exhibition for the attempt and $10,000 to finish.

Marilyn, sixteen years old and a petite five-foot-one, 110 pounds, vowed to last longer than Chadwick. Only a month before, she had been the first female to finish a 25-mile ocean swim in Atlantic City. That marathon race, however, had been staged in daylight.

Plunging into Lake Ontario at 11:07 p.m. from a United States Coast Guard station, the first problem Bell had to conquer was her fear of the dark. Feeling very alone as she was unable to hear the boats around her, Bell followed the single bobbing light of the escort boat for hours. She was also unpleasantly startled when the first of several lamprey eels she would encounter during the swim, clamped onto her leg, and she slowed slightly before kicking it off.

At around 4 a.m., Gus Ryder, her coach for seven years, noticed that her spirits had dropped. "Marilyn, you've swum all night!" he told her. "If you can do that you can do all the rest. In another hour the sun will be up and it will be really nice." In the ensuing hours, Ryder would also cajole her with reminders of promises made to war veterans and handicapped children.

After fighting the darkness, winds, cross-waters and waves all night, Marilyn's face was haggard, the muscles around her mouth slack, and her eyes glassy. She was also being pulled off course. Meanwhile, Ryder had been informed that Chadwick had been pulled out of the water before daybreak because she was sick, after completing only fifteen miles. Ryder had decided to save this bit of news until Bell was about ready to give up. Now was obviously the time and he held up a blackboard which read "Flo Is Out." Marilyn rallied and continued on as the only swimmer left (Jerry Kerschner and Winne Ruth Leuszler had also dropped out).

An hour later, though, she was crying, gasping for breath and unable to move her legs because of a stomach ache that had been steadily growing worse. Ryder told her she could come out, but as she moved toward the boat, he noticed her legs were kicking again and motioned for the crew to pull away. She followed, still crying.

Throughout the day, Ryder used the chalkboard to keep Bell posted on the growing sum of money that awaited her as the city of Toronto awoke to her sensational struggle. Sometimes her legs would grow so heavy, they would drag behind her, only to suddenly appear on top of the water again. At other times, her left arm lagged, then up it would come, in a fine powerful arc. Occasionally, she would stop to regain energy with corn syrup, Pablum or

coffee. She actually fell asleep twice, although the brief dozing didn't halt her strokes.

Finally, the skyline of Toronto began to take shape and as Bell headed into the second night of the swim, she was surprised to find yachts, motorboats, official launches, sailboats, harbor tugboats, kayaks and rowboats following her. In the gruelling last few miles it seemed to the onlookers as if she were hardly making any progress at all.

When she was hauled into the boat at 8:10 p.m., after touching breakwater, Bell was only half-conscious and oblivious to the boisterous crowd of 250,000 who cheered along the shoreline. She had covered a zig-zag distance of 40 miles in 20 hours 59 minutes.

"I haven't got a stomach," she told Ryder, "but I'm all right," she added while her doctor shook his head, amazed that her blood pressure remained normal.

The next day, she awoke to international acclaim and $50,000 worth of gifts. Newspaper editors named her Canada's Woman of the Year in 1954 and again the next year, when she became the youngest person to swim across the English Channel. Marilyn Bell's last big swim was in August 1956 when she became the first woman to cross Juan de Fuca Strait from the United States to Vancouver Island.

Maurice Richard

THE ROCKET
BY TERRY SCOTT

On a mid-September day in 1960, Maurice Richard glared into a row of television lights with those coal-black eyes and told the world he was retiring as a National Hockey League player. But long after the Montreal Canadiens' jersey with the familiar number 9 made its last round of appearances on NHL rinks, the man known simply as The Rocket hasn't faded from public consciousness.

A quarter-century later, Richard still draws prolonged and emotional ovations when he returns to the Forum for ceremonial functions. Teenagers who never saw a Richard goal join in the tribute, obviously well briefed on The Rocket's exploits by their elders.

The nickname came from Ray Getliffe, a teammate, who saw the rookie go into orbit in Canadiens' practices and warned the other players: "Watch out for the Rocket."

Before the name caught on, Richard was known as Bones, because he seemed to break more of them than hockey sticks. In two seasons of senior hockey before joining the Canadiens in 1942, he broke an ankle and a wrist. He snapped the other ankle shortly after his NHL debut and dislocated a shoulder at the start of his second season.

"Maurice is probably too fragile to play in the NHL," said Canadiens coach Dick Irvin Sr.

When he left the game after 18 glorious seasons, Irvin's fragile right-winger held or shared 33 NHL records, including most goals in a single season—50 in 50 games in 1944–45—and most career goals—544—despite missing 172 games because of injuries.

In Stanley Cup play, his six over-time goals and 18 game-winners have yet to be surpassed and 25 years went by before Mike Bossey of the New York Islanders caught up with his career playoff goal-scoring record of 82.

Richard was among the top five goal-scorers in 15 of his 18 seasons, leading the league four times. He received 14 all-star nominations, eight to the first team.

One of his general managers, Tommy Gordon, once said: "I have never seen a better player than Richard from the blueline in."

In a 1944 Cup semifinal, he scored all five goals in a 5–1 victory over the Toronto Maple Leafs. The following December, after spending the day moving into a new home, he had five goals and three assists against the Detroit Red Wings.

Against the 1950–51 Red Wings, who had finished 36 points ahead of Montreal, the underdog Canadiens won their first two semifinal games at the Olympia, both on Richard goals in the third overtime period.

Then on April 8, 1952, came what Irvin described as "the most spectacular goal I've ever seen."

In the second period of the seventh game of a rugged semifinal against Boston, The Rocket was carried from the ice after he collided with one Bruin and struck his head violently against the knee of another. Several minutes later, after receiving six stitches to close a gash on his forehead, Richard returned groggily to the bench.

Below: One way to stop The Rocket

With four minutes remaining and the score tied 1–1, the bruised and bandaged Rocket insisted he was ready to play. He took a pass near his own net, bulldozed his way through the entire Boston team and backhanded the winning goal past goaltender Sugar Jim Henry.

Another dimension to the Richard story is reflected by the equivalent of 21 games that he spent in the penalty box during regular-season. Introverted and at times a brooder, he was notorious for his volcanic temper. Far from deploring the violence, many of his francophone supporters identified his on-ice frustrations with their own at a time of growing political ferment in Quebec. And Richard was aware of his wider role.

"The Rocket once told me that when he played he felt he was out there for all French Canadians," said Réjean Tremblay, a *La Presse* columnist.

This special relationship between Richard and many of his fans played a significant part in the chilling events at the Forum on St. Patrick's Day in 1955.

Four nights earlier, the Canadiens played the Bruins in Boston. They were nursing a two-point lead over Detroit and Richard led teammate Bernie (Boom Boom) Geoffrion by two points in the individual scoring race.

In the first period, Bruins defenceman Hal Laycoe caught Richard with a crunching bodycheck. There was a scuffle and Laycoe's

stick came up, striking Richard on the head and opening a cut that later required five stitches. Richard put his hand to his head and, as he said later, "when I saw the blood, I became furious."

He hit Laycoe on the shoulder and head with his stick. As teammates and linesman Cliff Thompson tried to restrain him, Richard lost his stick but recovered it and splintered the wood across Laycoe's back.

Thompson, who earned only $25 a game for his officiating duties, grabbed Richard from behind and wrestled him to the ice. When he regained his feet, Richard punched the official twice in the face.

He received a match penalty and the incident was referred to league president Clarence Campbell for fur-

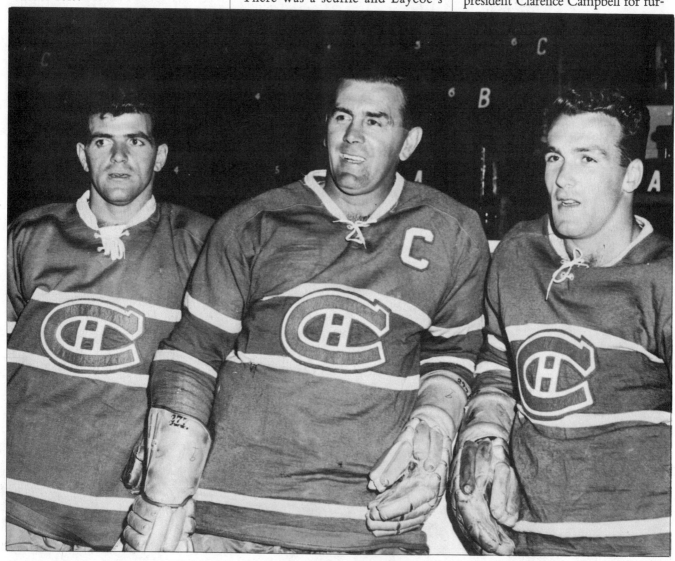

ther action. Three days later, the president suspended The Rocket for the last three regular-season games and the entire playoffs.

The next night, the Canadiens were scheduled to play Detroit in a showdown meeting at the Forum, prompting coach Irvin to remark to reporters, "I wonder if Mr. Campbell will be there. I certainly wouldn't want to be in his place if he sits in his usual seat."

It was clear in the hours leading up to the game that the public regarded Richard as a martyr. From the Saguenay district in the northern part of the province came a 5,000-name, 160-foot telegram of support. And there were warnings to Campbell on radio open-line shows that if he attended the game, he wouldn't leave the place alive.

Twice decorated for gallantry and a recipient of the ribbon of the Member of the British Empire for his services as a Canadian soldier in the Second World War, Campbell had obviously handled adversity. But as the final hours to game time approached, there were indications the Rhodes scholar was facing an unpleasant situation.

Early in the afternoon, the first group of placard-wavers arrived, displaying signs which read "Vive Richard!" and "Dehors (Down with) Campbell!" Others were even more uncomplimentary, showing a caricature of a pig bearing the name Campbell.

As the game moved past the tenth minute, there was a conspicuous pair of empty seats in the southeast corner of the Forum. Suddenly, the arena was filled with the sound of "Shoo, Campbell!" as the league president, sporting a grey fedora, and

accompanied by his secretary, Phyllis King, whom he married later that year, took his seat.

It wasn't long before the stoic Campbell was pelted with a stream of fruit, vegetables, eggs, rubbers and coins.

At the end of the first period, Campbell remained in his seat, and was in the process of rising to acknowledge the handshake of a black-jacketed youth, when the

"well-wisher" delivered a hand-slap to his face.

"He worked at Dow Brewery," Richard said years later of the lad. "I was told the plan was to grab Campbell and take him out on the ice, strip off his clothes and parade him around the ice in his undershorts."

As police moved to collar Campbell's tormentor, a tear gas bomb was set off in another section, envelop-

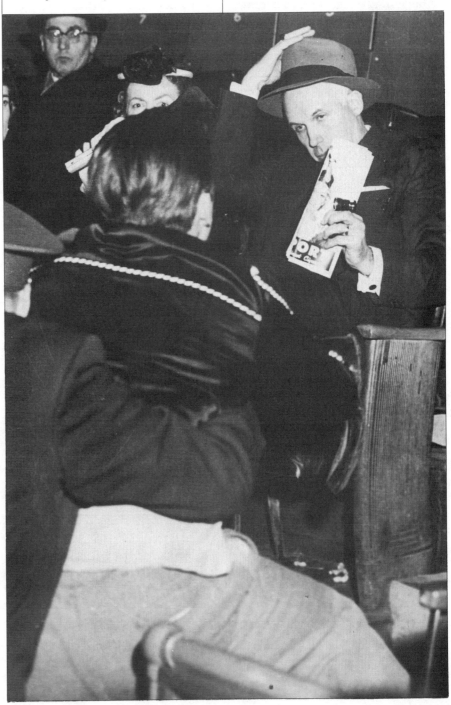

Left: The Richard Brothers—Claude, Maurice and Henri—in 1959

Right: Clarence Campbell under attack

ing the crowd of about 15,000 in a cloud of smoke.

Among those caught in the ensuing chaos was Raymond Paré, the city's fire chief, who couldn't get into the Forum because there was a crush of people trying to enter the building from the street to grab Campbell.

Once inside, Paré went to Canadiens general manager Frank Selke and told him he had the authority to stop the game, which he did, causing Montreal to lose by forfeit, 4–1.

Surprisingly, the Forum was calmly and swiftly evacuated, but on St. Catherine Street, the gathering mob turned ugly. Some of them jumped on the roofs of cars, while others

smashed the glass of the Forum entrance and upended newsstands and telephone booths.

The procession of rioters continued for several blocks along St. Catherine Street, some of them breaking windows and others scooping up the loot from the 50 shops that were victimized. At the police station the next day, a youngster emptied watches and rings from his pocket, and told police, "I still don't know why I did it, except that mob fever must have bitten me."

Fortunately, there were no deaths during the five-hour debacle, and the only injuries suffered were superficial. Police made 70 arrests, but 33 people were released. The average

age of those detained for petty crimes and public mischief was 19. Damages were estimated at more than $100,000.

The next afternoon, Richard called Selke and asked to make a television and radio appeal to the fans. With the Canadiens' dressing room as the setting, a sombre Richard said, "So that no further harm will be done, I would like to ask everyone to get behind the team and help the boys to win from the Rangers and Detroit."

Below: Richard celebrates his 500th goal

Right: The Rocket displays his famous temper

The fans heeded Richard's plea and calm was restored in the city, but his teammates, after beating New York on Saturday night, lost the regular-season crown to Detroit on Sunday. And Geoffrion, with Richard on the sidelines, edged Richard by one point for the scoring title.

"To give you an idea of Rocket's importance in the eyes of the fans, I got letters threatening my whole family because I won the scoring championship," Geoffrion recalled recently. "They even threatened to blow up my house."We had to have the house under police surveillance right into the summer."

Thirty-five years later, Richard admitted he was still troubled by the suspension.

"Some nights, before I go to sleep, I still think about it, and I have trouble getting to sleep. I have no animosity toward anyone, but I can't forget what happened.

"I still believe that what happened to me was unjust.

"I never expected it to be that large," Richard added, referring to the demonstration of displeasure by the fans on March 17, 1955. "After a few minutes that night at the Forum, I wanted the whole thing to end."

Obviously, Richard underestimated just how large a public figure he had become.

Below: Richard and Jean Beliveau with the 1958 Stanley Cup

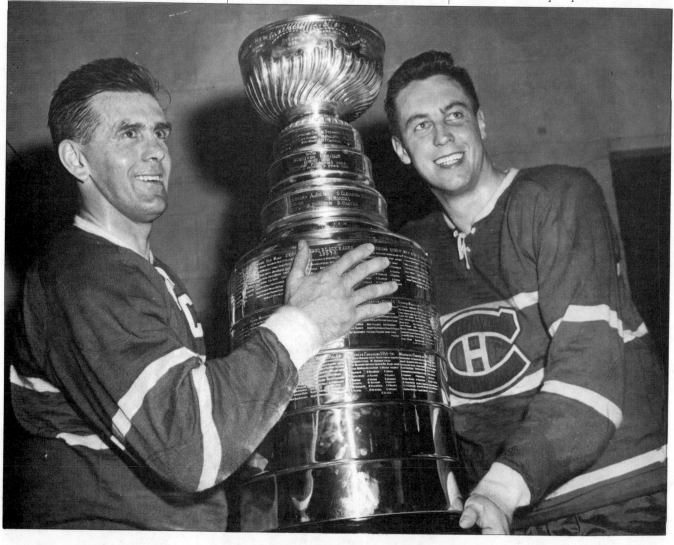

Coxless Four

THE STUDENT OARSMEN
BY CRAIG SWAYZE
THE ST. CATHARINES STANDARD

There have been many upsets in the history of international rowing. But few have matched the stunning performance turned in by the four fresh-faced University of British Columbia students who captured Canada's first gold medal in the sport at the 1956 Summer Olympics.

When coach Frank Read put his coxless four together that spring, Lorne Loomer, Walter d'Hondt and Archie McKinnon had never held an oar before. The only experienced member of the crew, Don Arnold, had to change sides when he was shifted into the stroke seat four months before the Olympics, one of the most difficult adjustments in rowing.

At the 1956 Olympic Trials in St. Catharines, Read's untried foursome won by ten lengths over challengers from Brockville, Winnipeg and Ottawa, covering the 2,000-metre course in an eye-opening six minutes 23.1 seconds. That was 13 seconds under an Olympic record that had stood since 1928.

But Read, a hard-driving disciplinarian, knew a fast time against unranked opponents offered no guarantee of success against the seasoned oarsmen his young crew—average age 20—would face in Australia. Relentlessly, he continued to urge them on to greater efforts.

At Lake Wendouree, 110 kilometres west of Melbourne, the Canadians won their opening heat over Germany, Australia and Denmark by four lengths in 6:36.6. Three days later they won their semifinal in 7:47.7 against a stiff headwind, defeating France, the Soviet Union and Poland by more than 20 seconds.

The final the next day was no contest. The superbly conditioned Canadians sprinted across the finish line in 7:08.8, five lengths ahead of the United States. France was third, another two lengths back, and Italy, the European champions, trailed the four-boat field.

"I think it can safely be said that they won as handily as any crew at any Olympics in the past," said Jack Guest Sr., a former Diamond Sculls champion and Olympic sculler who was manager of the 1956 Canadian rowing team.

Read's assessment of the victory was a summation of his coaching philosophy. "I don't pretend to know all the answers," he said. "But I do know that whatever your goal, be it high scholastic standing in university or success in your economic and social life, even the successful representation of your country in the Olympics, there must be self-discipline, determination and faith. And this sport of rowing does help develop those characteristics."

Robert Hayward

THE MAN WHO LOVED FAST BOATS
BY ROSS HOPKINS
THE CANADIAN PRESS, TORONTO

The first time Robert Hayward sat behind the wheel of Miss Supertest II, and experienced the exhilaration of flying down a stretch of calm water at more than 240 kilometres an hour, he forgot about racing anything else.

"It was love at first sight," he said after climbing into the cramped cockpit of Miss Supertest II that July day in 1957 and opening the throttle on the 2,000-horsepower Rolls-Royce aircraft engine.

Bitten by the speed bug at the age of fourteen, Hayward got his start racing outboard motor boats on the Thames River near London, Ontario. He then switched from water to land and took up drag racing until May 1957, when Miss Supertest II's

owner, Jim Thompson, asked him to join the crew as a mechanic. Three months later, he was at the controls full time and that summer established a world speed record of 296.99 kilometres per hour.

Hayward was short, stocky and very unathletic-looking, despite the fact it took great strength to keep the monster racing boats under control. He appeared an unlikely character for such a risky business, but speed and danger didn't bother him.

The following year, Thompson, president of the London-based Supertest Petroleum Corporation, decided to build Miss Supertest III, a nine-metre craft of laminated cherry plywood that Hayward would steer to three successive Harmsworth

Trophy victories. The hull sat two centimetres out of the water, riding on two sponsons protruding from the hull.

Hayward first won the Harmsworth in 1959, beating the American defender, Maverick, driven by William Stead. The event was a best-of-three series. Each race consisted of fifteen laps over a five-kilometre triangular course. Hayward won the first race when Stead ran into engine problems. The defender won the second, however, outmanoeuvring Hayward at the first turn and maintaining a small lead throughout.

In the decisive third race, Hayward changed his strategy and caught Stead by surprise at the start. Hayward drove Miss Supertest III into the far north corner of the course for his starting run, so he could pound the throttle and take a straight high-speed charge for the start line. He caught Maverick napping as Stead, unwilling to stray too far from the line, was coming out

of a circle to approach the start. Hayward broke the line just as the starting cannon was fired and Stead never recovered, his boat finally going dead in the water on the twelfth lap. The Harmsworth was Hayward's and he successfully defended it against U.S. challengers the following two years at Picton, Ontario, on the Bay of Quinte.

Then, on September 6, 1961, while racing Supertest II in the Silver Cup Regatta on the Detroit River (Supertest III raced only in Harmsworth competition), Hayward was killed. He appeared to have run out of both running and passing room when the two leading boats slowed for a turn. In a desperate effort to avoid a collision, Hayward swung sharply to the right at high speed, and his left sponson ripped into the water causing a sudden deceleration. The boat gyrated out of control and appeared to flip over, snapping Hayward's neck.

Don Wilson, driver of Miss U.S. I, one of the two boats Hayward was attempting to overtake, gave this description of the incident: "Bill Muncey (driver of Century 21) and I were battling into the first turn. We went into it at 225 kilometres per hour. The water was rough and we had less than six metres between us. So I drifted a little to the outside as a safety measure. As we neared the second buoy, our speed dropped to about 216 kilometres per hour. That is when I first saw Miss Supertest. She came right over our left sponson as if she was airborne and really flying. Hayward must have been doing 260. He appeared to be fighting for control as the boat bounced from one side to the other. I knew we were in trouble and I ducked down into my cockpit."

The first to reach Hayward was Bud Saile, driver of the trailing boat, Independent. He dived into the water and swam over to Miss Supertest, where he found Hayward lying unconscious in a twisted mass of wreckage. Efforts by doctors and fire department officials to revive him were unsuccessful and he was pronounced dead in the pit area.

Following the tragedy, Thompson retired the racing team and Miss Supertest III never raced again. The boat is on permanent display at the Ontario Science Centre in Toronto.

Left: Hayward pushes Miss Supertest III to full throttle

The Legendary Richardsons

BY BOB HUGHES
THE REGINA LEADER-POST

On a warm, soft summer day in June 1985, a distinguished-looking man in his fifties, sat having a quiet breakfast in the elegant Hotel Saskatchewan in Regina. As people came and went, it became obvious from their stares that many recognized the man immediately. Others walked to the table, shook hands and chatted for a few minutes. In a room which held prominent businessmen, politicians and Saskatchewan's beloved Roughriders, the tall man seemed to attract the most attention. This man, one could easily conclude, was somebody special.

A quarter-century after the end of his competitive curling career, Ernie Richardson's popularity is undiminished in Regina and throughout the province. Wearing Saskatchewan's colors, Ernie skipped the Richardsons to five provincial, four Canadian and four world curling championships, running up a record no rink has ever equalled. The world titles came in 1957, 1960, 1962 and 1963. In the first three, he teamed up with brother Sam, and cousins Arnold and Wes Richardson. For the fourth, Mel Perry replaced Wes, who had suffered a career-ending back injury.

Saskatchewan has always warmly embraced curling. Although a game which commands great skill, it is also a game which is played at a leisurely pace. Perhaps its popularity in Saskatchewan grew from the need of those in rural areas to kill off the long winters, when there were no crops to tend. Country curling rinks became the focal point for the social life of small-town Saskatchewan.

In the bigger cities, too, curling appealed to athletes looking for a way to keep active in the harsh Saskatchewan winters, which often last almost half a year. The Regina curling clubs, scattered about the city, became places where friends could meet, enjoy a game and then retire to the lounges or coffee shops to debate the wisdom of their playing strategy.

Over the decades, the province's curlers have tended to dominate or be near the top of the national curling scene. If the famed Garnett Campbell rink of Avonlea, a small town near Weyburn, put Saskatchewan curling on the map, then it was the Richardsons of Regina who ensured that it would stay there. And yet they seemed an unlikely group to forge such a remarkable trail of achievements in world curling history.

It was not until Ernie was twenty-one years old that he began to curl. And it was simply for the fun of it that he, Sam, Wes and Arnold threw together a rink in the winter of 1953. The last thing on their minds was the possibility that one day they would be sliding out of the hack in a rink in Scotland, the motherland of curling, to drift a rock down the ice in a world championship game.

But once they got their feet wet, the game gripped them. They couldn't get enough of it and they became not only addicts but students and inventors as well.

As soon as they finished a game at the Regina Civil Service Club, which later became the Regina Curling Club, the four would cluster together, poring over the game they had just played. They would analyse every end, every shot, every decision made by skip Ernie. At times, the discussions would grow heated. But it was all in the family, so nobody minded.

"I curled seventeen years with Ernie," recalls Sam, the comic of the group, and a man who is still much sought after as a sports dinner speaker. "During that time we only had two fights. And Ernie won them both. You know Ernie—he's big. It took a couple of beatings, but I learned."

Six years after they took up the game, the Richardsons won the inaugural world championship—the Scotch Cup. The initial world championships were best-of-five series spread out over a variety of Scottish curling clubs. Despite their unfamiliarity with the Scottish rinks, the Richardsons shocked the natives by

Below: The Richardsons

Right: The Richardsons with the MacDonald Brier Trophy

going through the first two tournaments undefeated.

"In our first game," recalled Ernie, "I threw my last rock through the house and blanked the end. I heard this old Scottish man say, 'Why, that's nae curlin'!' The Scots, especially the oldtimers, believed that a lot of rocks should be in play. Our game was hitting and they weren't really used to that. They just kept drawing, and we kept hitting."

The Richardsons had never travelled outside of Canada until their Brier victories propelled them to Scotland. And it was a whole new world for them. "There were no dividers on the ice," said Ernie. "There was no color in the rings. There were no hacks, so they had to nail them to the ice for us. It was different, but it was still curling."

The Richardsons bridged the gap between Canadian and Scottish curling without missing a beat. They wowed the Scots with their brilliant shotmaking and innovative strategy and even today you will find those who believe the Richardsons changed the face of curling. And late at night, in smoke-filled rooms where the curling fraternity gathers, there are many who maintain that Ernie was the greatest skip who ever played the "roaring" game.

The memories of those four world championships have stayed with the Richardsons, as crystal clear as if it had all happened yesterday. "It's sort of funny," Sam will tell you in his raspy voice. "We didn't get into the game to win any championships. Well, boy, once we played it we knew we liked it and we got serious. But we always had fun. We met so many great people, people we still know today. It was the socializing

that I liked the most, I think."

The attention paid to the Richardsons in Scotland was lavish. "You would have thought we were kings," laughs Sam. They were chauffeured about in Rolls-Royces and Bentleys and their every wish was granted.

There were also some startling moments during their tours of Scotland. Sam remembers one day when the rink went out to inspect the curling club on which the world championship would be played. "I looked out on the ice and there were about 1,500 kids skating around to Elvis music—they were having a hell of a time. I says to our guide, 'Where's the curling rink?' He points to the kids and says, 'Out there.' They had just flooded the ice over, drew out the rings and brushed out the rocks." In Canadian clubs, the sight of children skating

on the pebbled curling ice would set back the curlers a good century or two. But it didn't bother the Richardsons.

During the first three world championships they won, the Richardsons were largely known for their hitting game. Mel Perry remembers his world championship with the Richardsons in 1963. "By the time I got there," said Perry, "most teams were used to the Richardson style. The Scottish rink went to the hitting game almost too much. They started hitting everything in sight —biters, guards, everything. They forgot that we could play the draw just as well as we could hit."

When he looks back on the four world championships, Ernie labels the 1963 one—the last—as his most memorable. That year, the Richardsons and Perry were unbeatable. They were undefeated in the Saskatchewan playdowns, winning all 19 games they played. They won every bonspiel they entered, pulling in $20,000 in prize money. They figured they played over 100 games that winter and lost only about six. "To this day," Perry said, "I'll meet somebody who asks me if I'm the same guy who used to curl with the Richardsons. To this day, curlers still know our names."

The Richardsons were always welcomed royally when they returned home to Regina after their world championships. Crowds and parades awaited them as they stepped off the airplane, City Hall held special ceremonies and the provincial legislature would hold special sessions to honor them.

In 1975, Ernie was named to the Order of Canada. "Ernie called all of us and said he was going to turn it down," said Sam. "He said it was a team sport and he would feel bad accepting the award in only his name. I said, 'Don't be crazy, Ernie, you're representing our country—we all understand.'" Sam and the rest of the rink managed to talk Ernie into accepting the award.

Although only Sam continues to curl competitively, the Richardsons' legacy to Saskatchewan sport will always be remembered. The team has been selected to three halls of fame —the Saskatchewan Sports Hall of Fame in Regina, the Canadian Sports Hall of Fame in Toronto, and the Canadian Curling Hall of Fame in Winnipeg. And most weeks of the year, you can almost be assured of running into one of the famous curlers somewhere in Regina.

Below: Skip Ernie Richardson demonstrates his renowned accuracy. A light has been attached to the rock so that time exposure photography can trace its path

Right: Harry Jerome

Harry Jerome

THE MAN WHO MADE IT ALONE

BY NEIL DAVIDSON

THE CANADIAN PRESS, TORONTO

He ran like the wind, but sometimes it seemed to be an ill wind blowing when Harry Jerome laced up his track shoes. A sprinting legend, Jerome was the only man to hold world records in the 100-metre and 100-yard dash at the same time; winner of an Olympic bronze and British Empire Games gold; a world-class sprinter for the better part of a decade. But for every success there were equally bitter failures.

He was born on July 15, 1940, in Prince Albert, Saskatchewan, the fourth of five children. His father was a railway porter; his grandfather an Olympic sprinter. Jerome was a nineteen-year-old student at the University of Oregon when he burst onto the national scene on July 15, 1960, with a stunning performance at the Canadian Olympic trials at Saskatoon. He ran the 100-metre dash in ten seconds flat, tying the world record set less than a month earlier by Armin Hary of West Germany.

The performance took Jerome to the 1960 Rome Olympics where he broke the Olympic 100-metre mark of 10.3 seconds in the heats, but injured a muscle in the semifinal and was forced to the sidelines. Two years later, he held a share of the 100-yard dash world record at 9.2 seconds, but succumbed to injury at the British Empire Games in Perth, Australia. He had an infected throat, later diagnosed as tonsillitis, and a leg injury that proved to be career-threatening.

The press was unforgiving when Jerome pulled up lame, hinting he had folded once again. ''Jerome's shocking humiliation when he finished dead last in the British Empire

Games 100-yard dash final clouded what would have been Canada's finest hour Saturday in bigtime international competition since the Second World War,'' wrote Jack Sullivan of *The Canadian Press*.

The leg injury forced Jerome to spend months in hospital and then on crutches. Doctors believed he might never run again, but he returned in 1964 for the Tokyo Olympics after a controversial performance at the Canadian Olympic Trials in St. Lambert, Quebec. ''He virtually refused to try for good times, ran the heats and semifinals from a standing start, wearing sweatpants and sunglasses,'' one Toronto paper noted.

He came fourth in the 200-metre race in Tokyo and won an Olympic bronze medal in the 100 metres. "I was determined to win something this time," he said.

Jerome went on to win a gold medal in the 100 yards at the British Empire Games in Kingston, Jamaica, in 1966, the same year he ran 100 yards in 9.1. "Nobody yelled 'quitter' this time," Sullivan wrote.

Jerome returned in 1968 for his third Olympics, placing seventh in the 100-metre sprint. He retired that year and moved into sports administration, both provincially and federally. Many of the programs he developed are still in place, including plans to promote fitness at the elementary school level. He also cajoled levels of government to improve their minority rights programs.

Jerome was forty-two when he died of a brain seizure in 1982. "He turned magically from the quitter of the early '60s to be the hero that the press and (track) officials always expected him to be," Jack Batten wrote. "They were right at last but it wasn't their triumph or Canada's. Jerome made it alone."

Don Jackson
A MIRACULOUS PERFORMANCE
BY MEL SUFRIN
THE CANADIAN PRESS, TORONTO

On the night of Thursday, March 15, 1962, 18,000 figure-skating fans jammed Fucik Hall in Prague, Czechoslovakia, hoping home-town favorite Karol Divin would win the world championship. Divin led Donald Jackson of Oshawa, Ontario, by a whopping 45 points after the compulsory figures, and the experts knew it would take a miraculous free-skating performance for Jackson to win the title.

The twenty-one-year-old Canadian was the sixteenth skater. Because he had stayed in the dressing room while Divin skated, he had no idea what his opponent's marks were. As he prepared to skate, his coach, Sheldon Galbraith, who had

also coached Barbara Ann Scott to consecutive world titles and the Olympic gold medal in 1947 and 1948, said: "Don, there's room at the top."

"That's all I wanted to know," Jackson replied.

Then he proceeded to skate the performance of his life—five minutes of perfection during which he completed twenty-two jumps without a flaw, including the first triple Lutz ever performed in competition. Still, the question remained. Would the judges recognize what was obviously the greatest exhibition of free skating ever?

First came the marks of artistic impression—seven 5.9s, one 5.8

from the Canadian judge, and a perfect 6.0 from the West German. Then the scores for technical merit—one 5.8, again from the Canadian judge, two 5.9s and six 6.0s. The crowd, which had cheered throughout the remarkable performance, exploded with a roar of excitement, realizing it had witnessed a remarkable feat.

Still to come was Alain Calmat of France, also with a chance to win. But this was to be Jackson's night. When the final order of finish was announced, he was the gold-medal winner, with Divin second and Calmat third.

"He was fantastic," said Divin, who had offered to give Jackson his gold medal if, after the Canadian's brilliant performance, Divin had still emerged the winner.

No one had ever earned seven 6.0s in world competition before but that's what Jackson needed to win. There was disappointment in Fucik Hall, of course, because Divin had lost what had seemed to be an insurmountable lead. But it was overridden by the emotion one feels upon witnessing a moment of greatness. "It reduced everyone to a limp rag," wrote Alan Weeks, a Briton who described the event as "perhaps the greatest emotional moment in sport I have ever experienced."

Fog Bowl

THE TWENTY-FIVE HOUR GAME
BY MEL SUFRIN
THE CANADIAN PRESS, TORONTO

Sure, baseball games are sometimes postponed on account of rain, and hockey games have even been cancelled because of a snowstorm. But calling a football game because of fog? Incredible. Yet it happened.

It was Saturday, December 1, 1962, and Exhibition Stadium on the shore of Lake Ontario was enveloped in a real pea-souper, an odd contrast to the sunshine bathing the northern part of Toronto a few miles away. There were 32,655 spectators in the stands to watch the Winnipeg Blue Bombers play the Hamilton Tiger-Cats in the Grey Cup game but, with the fog occasionally settling almost to field level, few could say they were seeing the whole game.

Roof-level television cameras played peek-a-boo for a while before the networks decided to rely on equipment at ground level. ABC had paid $45,000 to televise the game in the United States and Canadian Football League officials were reluctant to postpone it because ABC said it was not sure it could show the game on Sunday. But they wouldn't admit that this was a consideration.

The game went on, and Garney Henley sprinted 74 yards down the sideline to give Hamilton a 6–0 lead in the first quarter. Leo Lewis, the Lincoln Locomotive, scored the first of his two touchdowns, then Charley Shepard caught his first touchdown pass in six years, Gerry James converting both, to put Winnipeg ahead 14–6 in the second quarter.

Touchdowns by Henley and Bobby Kuntz, the latter converted by the usually reliable Don Sutherin, gave Hamilton a 19–14 lead but a converted touchdown by Lewis made it 21–19 for Winnipeg. Dave

Viti put Hamilton into the lead, 26–21, in the third quarter, but Shepard's second touchdown made it 28–26 and a wide field goal attempt gave Hamilton a single. The third quarter ended with Winnipeg ahead 28–27.

With nine minutes 29 seconds left in the fourth quarter, the visibility, never more than 75 to 80 yards, was down to 40 and the players were no longer able to follow punts or long passes. Referee Paul Dojack suspended play and CFL commissioner Sydney Halter consulted with the teams' general managers. The decision was made to put off the remainder of the game until Sunday.

Next day, the fog was gone, although the skies were overcast, and about 15,000 fans showed up. With the Blue Bombers reeling from injuries suffered on Saturday, the Tiger-Cats completely outplayed them but never got quite close enough to kick the tying or winning points because of penalties and missed passes. With a limping Joe Zuger and Frank Cosentino sharing the quarterbacking duties for Hamilton, and Kenny Ploen playing both offence and defence and being spelled at quarterback by Hal Ledyard for Winnipeg, the Tiger-Cats outgained the Bombers in total yardage 489 to 366. But 90 yards in penalties for Hamilton against 35 for Winnipeg, combined with misses by Sutherin on two converts and two field goals, made the difference.

Winnipeg won its fourth national championship in five years, 28–27, in a Grey Cup game that took twenty-five hours to complete.

Right: Northern Dancer works out at Churchill Downs

Northern Dancer

WITH THE LOOK OF EAGLES
BY JIM COLEMAN

On the afternoon of Monday, February 24, 1964, I sat at a typewriter in the press box at Hialeah Park in Florida, tingling with excitement as I wrote of an extraordinary performance which I had witnessed a few minutes earlier: "A bull-chested colt sped through the sun-drenched homestretch at Hialeah today and rushed to the threshold of equine immortality.

"You can paste this warning in your hatband right now and refer to it on the afternoon of Saturday, May 2: Northern Dancer will be the first Canadian-bred to win the Kentucky Derby."

Northern Dancer's greatest achievements still lay ahead of him when those words were written but I make no claim to unusual prescience. Any man with an eye for equine grandeur would have discerned, immediately, that Northern Dancer was one of those rare superhorses "with the look of eagles."

In the ensuing twelve weeks, E.P. Taylor's feisty three-year-old went on an all-conquering six-race winning binge, during which he captured the Flamingo Stakes, the Florida Derby, the Blue Grass Stakes, the Kentucky Derby (in track-record time), and the Preakness Stakes. Then, Quadrangle and Roman Brother finished ahead of Northern Dancer in the Belmont Stakes to deprive him of the Triple Crown championship. Thereafter, The Dancer went home to Toronto and an easy victory in the 105th annual running of the Queen's Plate which was the final race of his brief, brilliant career.

A few weeks after the Queen's Plate, while the colt was at Belmont Park, training for a re-match with Quadrangle in Saratoga's Travers Stakes, he bowed a tendon in his left foreleg. To the lamentations of the entire Canadian nation, it was necessary to retire him to the breeding-farm. But, it was on the farm that he was to achieve even greater glory —he became the most successful stallion in North America.

But let's back up a bit: In the thoroughbred horse establishment which E.P. Taylor was operating in 1960, matings of expensive sires and mares were planned very carefully by Taylor and his bloodstock advisers, notably Joe Thomas who was manager of the Taylor equine enterprises. However, the mating which produced Northern Dancer was not embarked upon after a careful study of bloodlines, omens and auguries. Northern Dancer resulted from a "marriage of expedience": the mating of an unproven stallion named Nearctic and a very young mare named Natalma.

Nearctic, a Canadian-foaled speedster, was a good horse but not a great horse. When he ran, he carried his head too high and Taylor's Canadian trainer, Gordon "Pete" McCann, said ruefully that he resembled "an English carriage-horse."

Nevertheless, Nearctic could move very swiftly when the mood was on him. He set Canadian records for five furlongs and six furlongs but—most importantly for the purposes of this story—he won the $50,000 Michigan Mile in track-record time on Saturday, July 19, 1958. Taylor picked up a purse-cheque for $40,277 in U.S. funds.

Taylor, who raced his horses on both sides of the border, deposited the $40,277 in his U.S. account with the avowed purpose of spending that money for the purchase of a U.S. yearling at the auction sales which soon would open at Saratoga Springs in New York.

So, it is a matter of record that Taylor put a dent in Nearctic's Michigan Mile purse-money when he made a successful bid of $30,000 on Hip Number 213, a bay filly which had been sired by the outstanding grey race horse, Native Dancer. The filly, named Natalma, appeared destined for racing distinction, but things kept going awry for her. As a two-year-old, she finished first in the $50,000 Spinaway Stakes but she was disqualified when she body-checked another filly against the inner rails. In all, she won three of her seven starts and, as a three-year-old, she went to Churchill Downs as a prospective favorite for the Kentucky Oaks. A week before that important engagement, she broke a knee-bone.

Taylor called an emergency meeting at his Toronto home, summoning Joe Thomas and Horatio Luro, the trainer of Natalma and other Taylor horses which were racing on U.S. tracks. The topic for the emergency meeting: Natalma's future.

One alternative was to send the filly to the University of Pennsylvania where veterinarians were experimenting with a new type of surgery for knee fractures. Thomas pointed out that, up until that moment, such surgery had had very few successes. The other alternative was to breed Natalma, although she was only a three-year-old.

And what Taylor stud was immediately available? Well, there was Nearctic! It was strictly a gamble—Nearctic was standing his very first season on the farm and no one could guess whether he would sire good or bad horses. So, that was the way it was to be: Nearctic and Natalma. So much for scientific matings, carefully pre-planned by equine breeding pundits!

Natalma was delivered of her foal on May 21, 1961, at fifteen minutes after midnight. Peter Poole, who was alone with the young matron in the foaling-stall, wrote in the stable diary: "Tight but normal foaling." Although more than one hundred mares were foaling around the Taylor farm in those months, Poole recalled years later that Natalma's colt "always stood out a bit."

By September, Joe Thomas was chirping: "He's the best-looking yearling we ever had." Twelve months later, however, Thomas had changed his tune. Northern Dancer

had failed to grow as tall as his fellow yearlings. Thomas growled: "He was a real disappointment as a yearling. He was so short and so damned chunky—and he had cracked heels."

In that era, Taylor invited all his principal rival-owners to attend his annual sale. They were free to buy *any* of his yearlings at prices which were pre-designated by the Taylor bloodstock staff. Thus, in September 1962, Northern Dancer could have been bought for $25,000. However, his lack of height caused him to be dismissed by many very astute horsemen who appraised him. One wealthy owner had the grooms bring Northern Dancer out of his stall for inspection on three separate occasions, but he went away from the sale without making a purchase. Another owner had his trainer inspect Northern Dancer "from

stem to gudgeon;" he hemmed and hawed for an hour and, eventually, paid $25,000 for another colt who was taller and flashier than Northern Dancer.

One of the best bargains in the history of Canadian horse racing had slipped through the fingers of dozens of potential buyers. Northern Dancer stayed in the home-barn with the other horses of Taylor's Canadian division, trained by McCann.

McCann, Poole and all others who had early association with this remarkable colt, remember him ruefully as a rugged individualist with a highly irascible disposition. His handlers learned to be ready for quick, evasive action in his presence. Mouth open, he could lunge like a rattlesnake and, unexpectedly, lash out with his legs. Because it soon became apparent that Northern Dancer was the stable's rising star,

his handlers shrugged off his bellicose antics, saying: "He's just being playful." However, if he had been merely a cheap-selling plater, they would have described him as "a mean, rotten son of a buck."

The Dancer was brought along slowly because he had been a "late foal" and he was undersized. He didn't make his debut under silks until August 2 of his two-year-old season, at Fort Erie. He won his first race, finished second in his next start, and won the Summer Stakes at Fort Erie. He moved to Toronto where

Below: Northern Dancer runs away from the pack
Right: Willie Shoemaker aboard Northern Dancer

he had a second, followed by three successive triumphs, and trainer Luro took him to New York where he whipped some of America's best juveniles in winning an allowance-race and the Remsen Stakes at Aqueduct.

Before the running of the Remsen, the colt developed an ugly crack in his left forefoot. Luro took a calculated risk, wishing to test his precocious Canadian against the U.S. stars in this race. Fortunately, the crack in the hoof didn't spread during the running of the Remsen. Luro already had put in an emergency-call to Bill Bane, the celebrated California farrier. Bane, who had patented a process for patching cracked hooves with Neolite and quick-setting cement, flew to New York and spent an entire day vulcanizing the injured hoof. Thereupon, Northern Dancer was shipped to Florida to let his vulcanized hoof grow while he prepared for his date with destiny.

This brings us to the second start of The Dancer's three-year-old season, the performance which I described in the opening paragraphs of this story. In his only previous race of 1964, he had finished third to Chieftain in a six-furlong sprint, viewed primarily as a test for his repaired hoof.

Then, on that beautiful afternoon of February 24, he was running in an old-fashioned sporting trial—a race with no purse and no betting. The runners were three colts owned by millionaires and they were going seven furlongs in preparation for the following week's $100,000 Flamingo Stakes.

Northern Dancer's two rivals were Chieftain, owned by Raymond Guest, the U.S. polo star; and Trader, owned by Mrs. Charles Shipman Payson and her brother, John Hay Whitney. There was no purse at stake but the owners were shooting! Bill Shoemaker flew from California, just to ride The Dancer in the trial. Bill Hartack had the mount on Chieftain. John Rotz rode Trader. The race itself proved to be no contest. Northern Dancer simply ran away and hid on his two rivals. The Canadian bandwagon picked up a fresh load of converts as it prepared to roll on to Kentucky.

The one person whose usually sound judgment began to desert him that afternoon was William Shoemaker, the world's most successful jockey. Shoemaker already had made an informal agreement to ride Northern Dancer in the Kentucky Derby. However, when he dismounted from the Taylor colt after that trial race at Hialeah, The Shoe was oddly uncommunicative. Questioned by reporters, he professed to be satisfied and he told them that he would be coming back to Florida to ride Northern Dancer in the Flamingo and the Florida Derby.

Nevertheless, those who knew him well detected some hesitation in his manner. Shoemaker never would have admitted it publicly at that moment, but he suspected that two California colts—Hill Rise and The Scoundrel—were better than any East Coast three-year-olds. In his own interest, he was keeping his Kentucky Derby options open. And sure enough, after Shoemaker won the Flamingo and the Florida Derby on Northern Dancer, he begged off the Canadian colt for future engagements. Almost simultaneously, it was announced in California that Shoemaker had agreed to ride Hill Rise in the Kentucky Derby.

Although slightly miffed by Shoemaker's eleventh-hour defection, the Taylor establishment had no hesitation in signing up the brilliant, if occasionally moody, Bill Hartack. Trainer Luro, particularly, was hap-

py to obtain the services of Hartack who had won the 1962 Derby on Decidedly, trained by Luro.

On Saturday, May 2, when the field of twelve colts went to the post for the 90th annual running of the Kentucky Derby at Churchill Downs, Hill Rise was the favorite at 7 to 5. Northern Dancer was second choice at the rather attractive price of 7 to 2. The Scoundrel was third choice at 6 to 1.

A few frenzied minutes later, I was sitting at a typewriter, again pounding out these words: "The hero of this place is The Fastest Canadian on Four Feet. Northern Dancer, our pugnacious little horse with the musculature of a perfectly-conditioned heavyweight, ran a hole in the wind as he shattered the Kentucky Derby record for one mile and one-quarter." Back home in Canada, the millions who had watched the Derby on television, were all but dancing in the streets. Without question, it was the most important victory in the history of Canadian horse racing.

After the presentation ceremonies in the winner's enclosure, Northern Dancer was obliged to submit to the customary drug tests. Accordingly, it was 50 minutes after the race that a gnarled old groom, Will Brevard, finally led the colt back to his shedrow in the Churchill Downs stable area.

By that time, Northern Dancer's blanket of roses—and iced tubs of champagne—had been carried into the Taylor tackroom. In the ensuing half-hour, scores of ladies and gentlemen who had assembled for the stable-area celebration, emerged from that tackroom, clutching individual roses and full glasses of champagne. They stood in the late afternoon sunlight, watching the colt take his cooling-out walk under the gabled roof of the long barn.

It was Baylor Hickman, a tall, aristocratic Kentuckian, wearing a Black Watch tartan jacket, who pro-

vided the appropriate benediction. As Northern Dancer passed the tackroom door, Hickman raised his glass of champagne to the colt and loudly —so that everyone could hear him —cried: "The Maple Leaf Forever." The Derby field had gone to the post at 4:31 p.m. It was 6:15 p.m. when Northern Dancer completed his long walk and was led into his stall for the night. He didn't look tired—just rather pleased with himself.

Two weeks later, the Preakness Stakes at Pimlico resembled a rerun of the Derby although, this time, Northern Dancer wasn't forced to the limit. He deposed of Hill Rise and Quandrangle in the first six furlongs, and then romped along to win by more than two lengths, with The Scoundrel finishing second, while Hill Rise was third.

Even at the Preakness, the American racing public wasn't ready to concede that a Canadian-bred was superior to their homebred colts. They never had regarded Canada as a suitable breeding-ground for thoroughbred horses; southern horsemen still were deluded by the specious theory that snowbound Canada was more suitable for the breeding of bison, muskox and caribou. Therefore, in the Preakness, the public

made Hill Rise the odds-on favorite. Northern Dancer was only a lukewarm second choice at odds of better than 2 to 1. Ironically, the only Triple Crown race in which Northern Dancer went to the post as the favorite was the Belmont Stakes— which he lost!

In retrospect, the Belmont was an oddly-run race. Hartack, possibly under instructions to keep a close eye on arch-rival Hill Rise, had Northern Dancer under stout restraint in the early stages of the long run of one mile and a half. The Dancer didn't take kindly to those tactics. When Hartack finally gave him his head, the Canadian colt was lathered with the sweat of exasperation and he failed to display his customary dash. Quadrangle, who had been galloping along, never more than a length behind the pace-setting Orientalist, pulled away from the field on the final turn. Northern Dancer, tiring obviously in the hot, humid afternoon, was unable to save second place from the late-charging Roman Brother.

Right: Four-man bobsled roars around witch's curve

Despite the result of the Belmont, U.S. turf writers unanimously selected Northern Dancer as North America's three-year-old champion when they voted at the end of the 1964 season. After all, they were keenly aware that he had administered sound beatings to Quadrangle and Roman Brother in the Derby and in the Preakness. Taylor's bantam colt was hailed as a national hero when he came home to Toronto for the last race of his career, the Queen's Plate, on June 20. A crowd of 32,000 applauded him ecstatically as Hartack rode him to an easy victory over seven courageous but outclassed rivals. Northern Dancer wasn't merely hero-for-a-day. For more than two decades after his victories on the track, Canadians continued to glory vicariously in his achievements as his progeny established themselves as the best thoroughbreds in Europe, as well as in North America. He was, unquestionably, the most explosive and potent hunk of horseflesh ever to be born on Canadian soil. We shall be boundlessly fortunate and twice-blessed if ever we see his like again.

Bobsled

CANADA'S FIRST-TIME CHAMPION
BY CHRIS CARIOU
THE CANADIAN PRESS, WINNIPEG

Scrunched together for their first real run down the treacherous chute at the 1964 Innsbruck Olympics, four Canadian bobsledders had already come a long way in a short time. But, to the surprise of world bobsledding powers—Italy, Switzerland, Austria—and to the delight of a Canadian public, they were destined to go even further and much faster. Vic Emery and his brother John, along with teammates Doug Anakin and Peter Kirby, careered down the run in record time to give the unheralded Canadians their country's first Olympic bobsledding medal.

Canada had never even entered an Olympic bobsledding event before the foursome decided to become bobsledders. After the 1956 Olympics in Cortina d'Ampezzo, Italy, the group spent thousands of dollars to buy or rent sleds and other equipment, and to live in Europe where they could train with the best in the world. Fund-raising helped their cause and, by the early '60s, they were getting set for the Olympics. In the 1963 world championship, they placed ninth.

Somewhat in awe of the European teams before the Olympic training began, the Canadian squad gained confidence as they began to improve their time. "We had a start that was innovative," Anakin said. "We were doing the crouch start where you come out like a football player. Previously bobsledders used to rock and pull it, and half the teams were still doing that."

In the Olympic training run in Innsbruck, the Canadians were beating everybody. "We knew Vic was our best driver," said Anakin, the smallest member of the team at five-foot-seven, "and that he was up with the top six or seven in the world. We felt we had a chance."

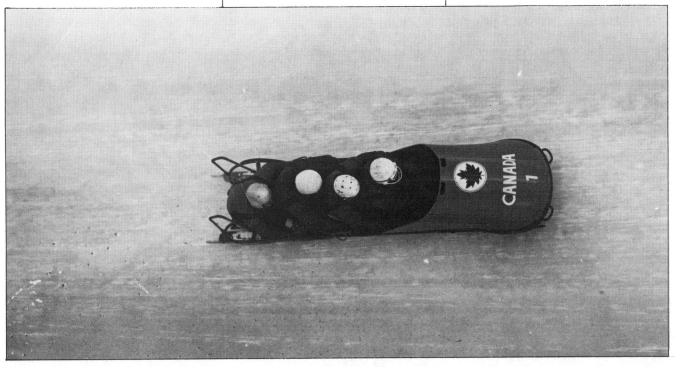

As it turned out, none of the other favored countries had much of a chance after the first of four heats. On their first run, the Canadians set a course record of one minute 2.99 seconds and led every other team by more than a second. The lead stood up into the fourth and final heat. The Canadians had to come up with another good run and then hope their more experienced opposition—mainly former world champion Eugenio Monti of Italy—wouldn't produce a miracle run to make up the margin.

"We realized, now it's serious," said Anakin. "We can't just think about bobsledding and then going for a ski in the afternoon and maybe win in some future year—we've got to do it now."

Although the Canadians had their slowest time on the final run, it was enough to sustain their one-second margin. While Vic Emery shook Monti's hand, the rest of the team rejoiced. Thinking back to less glamorous days for Canadian bobsledders, Anakin said it always seemed "you knew you were going to zig-zag and bang your way down the course and end up fifteenth or twentieth or something." But at Innsbruck in 1964, "we climbed right through that."

Nancy Greene
THE "GO-FOR-IT" GIRL
BY RON SUDLOW
THE CANADIAN PRESS, VANCOUVER

Ski Queen, Nancy Greene. It was a favorite sports page phrase. It rolled off the tongue as smoothly as a carved turn through a slalom gate.

However, on the slopes Greene was called "The Tiger" for the go-for-it style that brought her consecutive World Cup titles in 1967 and 1968, plus gold in the giant slalom and silver in the slalom at the 1968 Winter Olympics in Grenoble, France.

Now a forty-two-year-old mother of twin teenaged boys, Greene recalls learning to ski early in her own childhood in the tiny mining town of Rossland, British Columbia. She started on homemade skis at the age of three when her father Robert, an engineer, would sit her on his knee as they rode up the lift at Red Mountain, a snowball's throw from their home. Red Mountain is so steep that the Greene kids learned the sport with a rope tied around their waists. If they fell, Father would reel them in. "We skied all over the place, especially through the funny little trails, the dips and jumps and bumps through the woods. Just skiing down the hill was a little boring because I liked to go fast and wasn't scared of the slope."

Greene, a national team member from 1959 to 1968 and six-time Canadian champion, impressed coaches at fourteen when she got into a slalom at the Canadian junior championships after another skier suffered an injury in practice. She made her first Olympic team in 1960 and finished twenty-second in the downhill—second among Canadians—at Squaw Valley, California. She improved to seventh in the downhill and fifteenth in the slalom in 1964 at Innsbruck, Austria.

Right: Nancy Greene in full flight at Chamonix, France, 1968

*Ron Turcotte and Secretariat in the Winners
Circle at Churchill Downs, 1973*

Gaetan Boucher at Sarajevo, 1984

Ken Dryden covers up while a Soviet player looks for a rebound, 1972

*Canadian fans make their presence felt
in Moscow, 1972*

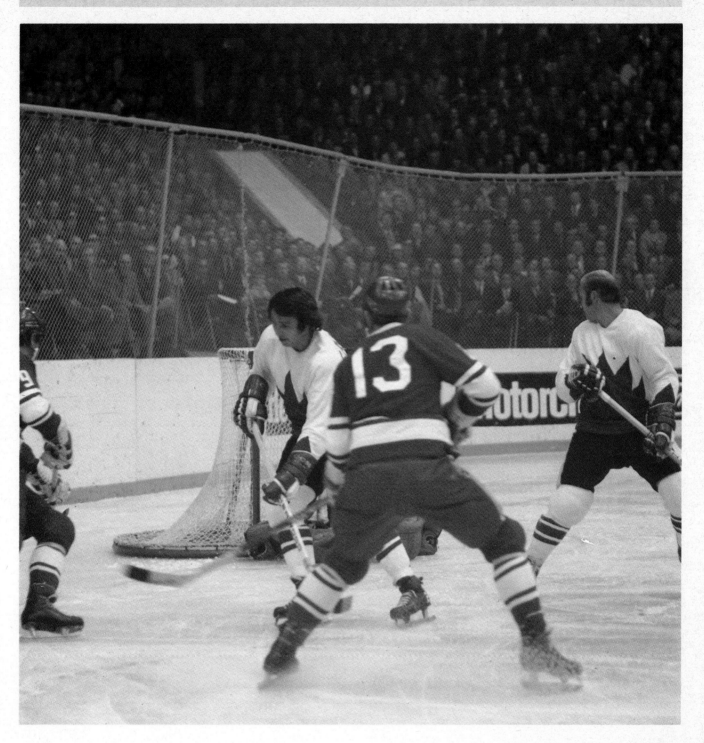

Brad Park and Bill White defend the Canadian net

*Peter Mahovolich dumps a Soviet player
behind the net*

Shawn O'Sullivan lands a left on Christophe
Tiozzo of France, 1984

Willie de Wit bounces a left off Arnold Vanderlijde of Holland

Edmonton Eskimos led by Dave Cutler's
kicking and Warren Moon's arm made the
Eskimos a devastating force

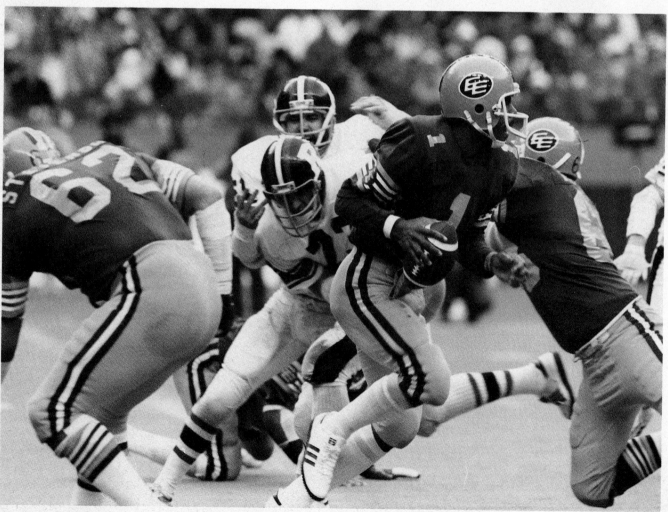

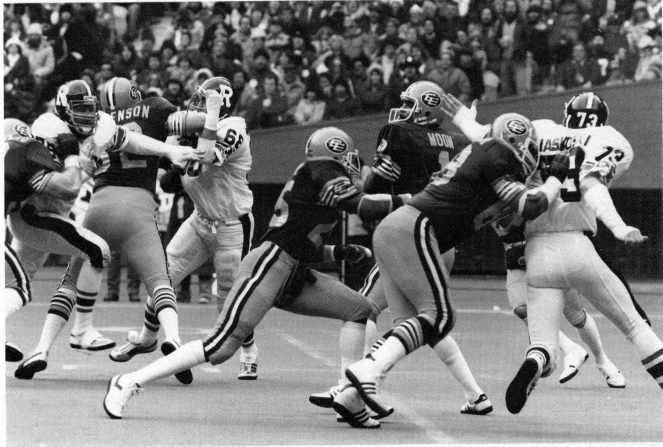

Gretzky — The Great One

Gretzky with the Art Ross Trophy (left), the Stanley Cup, and the Hart Trophy

*Alex Baumann celebrates a gold medal, and
a world record*

*Victor Davis pounds the water after finishing
the 200m breast stroke with a world record and
gold medal*

Anne Ottenbrite strikes gold in the L.A. games, 1984

Willie Huber ties up Guy Lafleur at the Forum

Guy Lafleur acknowledges the crowd's cheers

Gordie Howe and Larry Robinson tie each other up in a game at the Forum

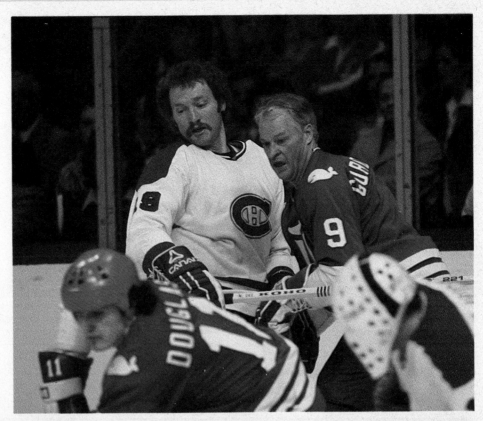

Bobby Orr and Gerry Cheevers try to stop Yvan Cournoyer

Gilles Villeneuve

Kathy Kreiner at Lake Placid, 1984

The Crazy Canucks: Ken Read, Steve Podborski, Dave Murray and Dave Irwin

Some of Montreal's all-time greats. (Left to right) Jacque Plante, Larry Robinson, Toe Blake, Jean Beliveau, Dickie Moore, Aurele Joliat, Doug Harvey, Rocket Richard, and Bob Gainey.

Jean Beliveau rounds the net

*Symbols of a continuing dynasty, Jean
Beliveau, Guy Lafleur and Rocket Richard*

Larry Robinson

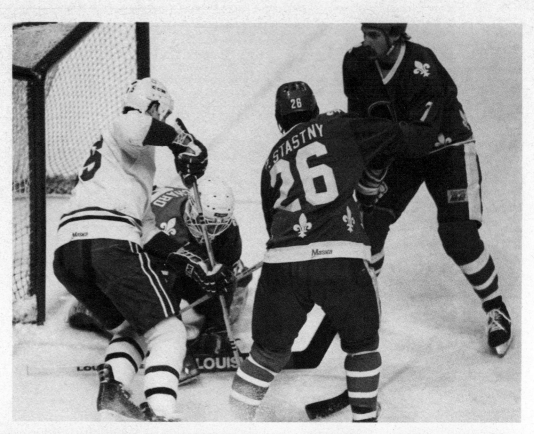

The rivalry between the Quebec Nordiques and the Montreal Canadiens makes each game 'the battle of Quebec'

Montreal's Mike McPhee avoids a check from
Quebec's Pat Price

The first World Cup competition was organized in 1967 and Greene won in a western-style showdown at the final meet at Jackson Hole, Wyoming. She trailed French skiers Marielle Goitschel and Annie Famose and needed to win the final three races. The first two were giant slaloms which she won easily. Then her nerves got the better of her. She stewed most of the night before the final slalom of the season. Although tired and tense, she placed second in the first run and relaxed to win the second, beating Goitschel by seven-hundredths of a second for the World Cup.

There was pressure of a different kind the next year when Greene had a big lead in the World Cup standings. A win would clinch her second title in front of family, friends and fans on Red Mountain, but racing before her parents for the first time since 1960, she had a painful wipeout in the second run of the slalom and injured her ankle and neck. Snow packed into her ski boot prevented swelling and a chiropractor manipulated two vertebrae back into place. Her luck changed for the giant slalom the next day when she drew the number 1 start position for an icy course that would become rutted and slower with each skier. She won by nearly two seconds.

There were fears that her tender ankle would prevent Greene from capturing Olympic gold. She started slowly at Grenoble with a tenth in the downhill, but a powerful second run brought silver in the slalom behind Goitschel. Then she thundered through the giant slalom to beat Famose by a whopping four seconds as she attacked the course from top to bottom.

Nancy Greene's success brought endorsements, public relations work and television appearances as a color commentator. She married national team coach Al Raine in 1969 and they are currently involved in real estate development at the Whistler ski resort near Vancouver.

Below: Nancy Greene wins the World Cup and is congratulated by France's Marielle Geitschel

Sandra Post

THE COMBATIVE GOLFER

BY IAN MACLAINE

THE CANADIAN PRESS, TORONTO

Even before Sandra Post joined the Ladies' Professional Golf Association (LPGA) tour in 1968, she had her troubles with the golfing establishment. Four years earlier, as a precocious sixteen-year-old, the Oakville, Ontario, girl was excluded from the provincial junior team. She responded by winning the Ontario junior title, followed by an eight-stroke victory for the first of her three national junior championships.

In 1967, she lost the amateur Doherty Cup individual title at Fort Lauderdale, Florida, to Alice Dye when the veteran American dropped a five-foot-par putt on the second playoff hole. Post turned the tables on Dye a few months later, defeating her 3 and 2 in the 36-hole, match play final of the South Atlantic championship at Daytona Beach, Florida. Some of Post's detractors, who deplored her lack of social graces, attributed the victory to "spite motivation." She preferred to call it "determination".

Whichever it was, Post's combative attitude carried over into her rookie season as a professional and barely mellowed throughout a career that ended when a nagging back injury forced her premature retirement in 1983. "I'm not a good loser," she admitted. "No good athlete is."

Not everyone was offended. When Post signed her temporary LPGA card and became Canada's first touring professional woman golfer, her early supporters included Kathy Whitworth, already earmarked for the LPGA Hall of Fame, and Marlene Stewart Streit, Canada's premier amateur golfer. "Now someone has taken the plunge, I think someone else might not be as reluctant," Streit said. And many Canadians have followed Post's trail, although none have come close to matching her achievements.

From the moment she teed up for her first tournament, the Orange Blossom Festival at St. Petersburg, Florida, in which she placed twentieth, it was apparent that she was something special. By her twentieth birthday, on June 4, she was already touted as the tour's outstanding newcomer.

In early April, at the Lady Carling tournament in Atlanta, she became the first tour player to break

30 for nine holes, scoring a 29. But it didn't count. Her playing partners hadn't noticed, but Post's overzealous caddy had put his hand on the putting surface to get the lie of the green. She penalized herself two strokes for the infraction and went on to shoot 68—the first time she had broken 70.

That was only the beginning. On June 25, Post carded eight birdies to defeat Whitworth, the defending champion, by seven strokes for the LPGA crown in an eighteen-hole playoff, including a 100-foot chip-in from off the green on the 16th hole. The chip unnerved Whitworth, who took a quadruple-bogey eight on the seventeenth hole and finished with a 75.

The win was worth $3,000, Post's biggest cheque of the year, and secured her status as the best newcomer of 1968, a position ratified in December when she was named Rookie of the Year by both the LPGA and Golf Digest. In twenty-six official tournaments that year, she placed in the top ten eight times and won $17,835—small potatoes by today's inflated standards but a rookie record at the time.

As the purses improved, Post's winnings increased to a career total of nearly $750,000. She won eight LPGA tournaments and was twice selected as Canada's woman athlete of the year.

Left: Sandra Post tees off

Elaine Tanner

MIGHTY MOUSE

BY NEIL STEVENS

THE CANADIAN PRESS, TORONTO

Elaine Tanner stood barely five feet tall and was only fifteen years old, but in August, 1966, she reached heights no Canadian swimmer had previously attained. The broad-shouldered Grade 10 student from Vancouver, nicknamed Mighty Mouse, won four gold and three silver medals at the Commonwealth Games in Kingston, Jamaica, a feat that led to her selection as the youngest winner of the Lou Marsh Memorial Trophy as Canada's outstanding athlete.

The memorable week for Tanner began when she teamed with Jane Hughes, Louise Kennedy and Marion Lay for a world-record victory in the 4 × 110-yard freestyle relay. It was the first major event of the Games and, for the first time, the new Canadian Maple Leaf flag was raised above the winner's podium at an international meet.

Tanner subsequently won the 220-yard butterfly and claimed silver medals in the 110 backstroke and 4 × 110 medley relay with teammates Kennedy, Lay and Donna Ross. On Friday, August 12, the final day of swimming events, a noisy contingent of Canadians cheered her on, chanting out M-I-G-H-T-Y M-O-U-S-E as Tanner raced through the water. Tanner won the 110 butterfly and the 440 individual medley and took silver in the 220 backstroke.

No woman, in any sport, had ever won as many medals in previous Commonwealth competition. At five-foot-two, 115 pounds, Tanner was smaller than most of her opponents, but she was more than a match for them in strength and determination. "She's the greatest swimmer Canada has ever produced," said coach Ted Simpson. "A

lot of it was born in her but her biggest asset is that she knows how to pull through the water. It's a sensory effect you must have over water. You must know you can control it. She has more power per pound than the other girls."

A year later, Tanner won two gold and three silver medals at the Pan-American Games in Winnipeg, smashing three world records. The new Olympic-sized pool was nicknamed "Tanner's Tank" after she began training in it under the direction of coach Howard Firby for the 1968 Summer Olympics in Mexico. She won two silver medals at the Games, but failed to win the gold medals she wanted most.

Tanner quit competitive swimming in 1979 at age eighteen. She was named to Canada's Sports Hall of Fame in 1971 and toured the country during the '70s, helping to raise funds for the national swimming team.

Below: Elaine Tanner heads for a world record in the 220 yard medley in 1966

Bobby Orr
REVOLUTION ON DEFENCE
BY GERRY SUTTON
THE CANADIAN PRESS, TORONTO

In playground hockey games twenty-five years ago, the best skaters were on the forward line, the bravest kid went into goal and the least-talented youngsters played defence. Then, suddenly, everybody wanted to be Bobby Orr.

Of course, there were talented defencemen in the National Hockey League before Orr came along— bruisers who would flatten an unwary attacker with a devastating hip-check, tacticians who steered him gently into a corner or finesse artists who poke-checked the puck off his stick and turned it over to a teammate. But a defenceman's top priority was to defend. The only offensive contributions expected of him were to head-man the puck to a forward and blast the occasional shot from the point on a power-play.

Coaches began to rethink that strategy in 1962 when a spindly fourteen-year-old defenceman from Parry Sound joined the Oshawa Generals of the Ontario Hockey League, one of the prime breeding grounds for the pros, and started skating rings around top NHL prospects who were three or four years older.

Probably no other player before or since has dominated a junior league as Orr did in his four years with the Generals, spearheading their offensive thrusts and reappearing magically to break up a play at the other end.

Still, there were plenty of skeptics when the Boston Bruins moved Orr into their lineup at the tender age of eighteen. The Bruins, who hadn't made the playoffs since 1959, needed all the help they could get. But the history of the game is well stocked with players who arrived in the NHL with awe-inspiring junior records, spent a year or two on the end of the bench, and wound up pumping gas or pitching hay after playing out the string in the minors.

To the delight of the victory-starved Boston fans, Orr proved to be a newcomer who lived up to his press clippings, baffling battle-hardened NHL veterans with the same tactics that had marked his junior career. In his first professional season, he was named rookie of the year and made the second all-star

Below: One of hockey's most famous moments—Bobby Orr scores the Cup winner, May 10, 1970

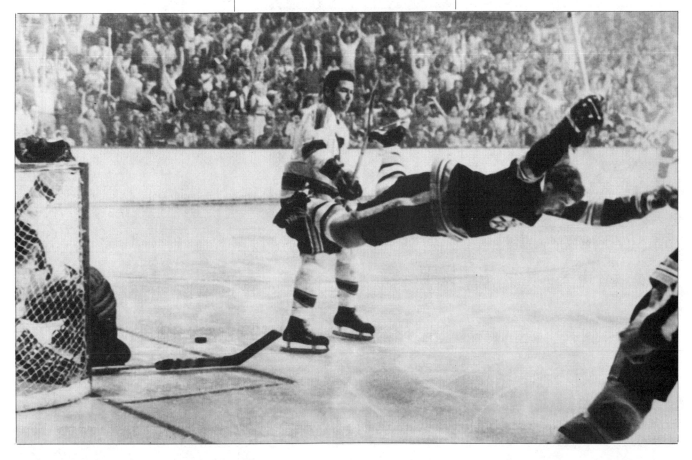

team. Over the next eight years, he led the team to two Stanley Cups and three divisional titles.

Eight seasons in a row, he won the Norris Trophy as the league's top defenceman. He led the league in scoring twice, was named Most Valuable Player three times, and set single-season and career scoring records for a defenceman before chronic knee problems forced him out of the game at the age of thirty.

The goal that won the Stanley Cup in 1970 was typical. The fourth and deciding game against the St. Louis Blues had gone into overtime with the score tied 3–3. The Bruins won the opening faceoff and applied relentless pressure in the St. Louis zone. Eventually, Orr got the puck on the boards, took a tremendous check that sent him flying in front of goaltender Glenn Hall, and still managed to nudge the puck home.

That season earned Orr four individual league trophies, two awards as Canada's athlete of the year and another as sportman of the year from the U.S. magazine *Sports Illustrated*.

Purists never stopped grumbling that his aggressive style left the team vulnerable in its defensive zone. But Brad Park, another all-star defenceman who played with and against Orr, had the definitive answer to that complaint. ''You don't have to play defence if you've always got the puck.''

Ferguson Jenkins

GOOD TIMES—BAD TIMES

BY EATON HOWITT
THE CANADIAN PRESS, TORONTO

Sure, Ferguson Jenkins has had his great moments, but right along with them have been some bad times. Let's take some of the great things first: Considered the best Canadian-born player ever to play baseball in the major leagues, he is only one of four pitchers to win more than 100 games in each league. He is also the only pitcher in baseball history to strike out more than 3,000 batters (3,192) and walk fewer than 1,000 (977).

Now forty-one and living on his Circle J Ranch in the farming community of Blenheim near Chatham, Ontario, where he was born, Jenkins recalls some of the bad times in his years with the Philadelphia Phillies, Chicago Cubs, Boston Red Sox and Texas Rangers.

Needless to say, he is a little upset that the year the Cubs let him go, they won their way to the World Series for the first time in thirty-nine years, just one year too late for him. The team's all-time strikeout leader and a 20-game winner for them each year from 1967–72 (he won the Cy Young award in 1971), he was released before the start of the 1984 season without ever reaching the playoffs or the series. He had also hoped that either the Toronto Blue Jays or Montreal Expos would pick him up, but they didn't.

While baseball was the big sport in his life, it was not the only one. A big chap (six-foot-five), he had a whirl at basketball with the Harlem Globetrotters, and hockey, once his first love, remains close to the top even today. He recalls that even hockey had its bad moments for him, though. While he was with the Texas Rangers in 1974–75, he was playing in an industrial league during the winter months at home. The Rangers were, of course, unaware that he was playing hockey or they would have made him quit. During a game, one of the opposition kept checking him. "I dropped my glove

and let him have it—bam—and broke all the knuckles in my right hand." It was his pitching hand, but it cleared up in time and that summer he pitched seventeen winners.

On August 25, 1980, just before the start of a three-game series between his Texas Rangers and the Toronto Blue Jays, bad times came again to the Canadian Sports Hall of Famer and several-time Canadian Athlete of the Year. He was taken from the stadium back to the airport and charged with three counts of possession of four grams of illegal drugs for personal use, found in his luggage.

Jenkins was suspended by Commissioner Bowie Kuhn. During the winter, he was found guilty but given an absolute discharge, which means he has no criminal record. During the trial, one after another of the people from the Chatham area gave character evidence and told of the baseball player's many good deeds, especially his work with young people. Jenkins said his encounter with the law on drug charges "was like running into a steel wall."

Incidentally, the day he was arrested was Jenkins' second trip back to Canada within the year. On his first trip, he was made a Member of the Order of Canada.

Typical Fergie Jenkins—the good mixed in with the bad.

Right: Harry Sinden watches the action carefully

1972 Hockey

THE CANADIAN-RUSSIAN SHOOTOUT
BY BRUCE LEVETT
THE CANADIAN PRESS, TORONTO

Great moments in sport generally come swiftly. A kid you never expected to win suddenly launches a flurry of left jabs and a star is born. A crew suddenly raises the beat and begins to pull away, and you know instantly that life will never be quite the same again for anybody in that boat. A spiralling football begins to drop and a figure swerves beneath it, reaching up, and suddenly you realize that here, too, is greatness. Suddenly. It's the way it generally happens.

But it wasn't quite like that in 1972 when Canada and the Soviet Union met in an eight-game shootout for the hockey championship of the world. It was more like a skyrocket that sputtered and rose slowly, gaining altitude to finally burst with a glare unexpected in its brilliance.

"We'll take these guys in eight straight," they quoted Phil Esposito as saying before the series. And Phil had a right to be confident. After all, hadn't he just led the Boston Bruins to the Stanley Cup? And wasn't he going into the series as the linchpin of probably the greatest all-star hockey team ever assembled?

Well, we didn't take those guys in eight straight. We did take them, but by one lone goal—scored in the dying seconds of the final game. This is, essentially, the story of that goal and how it came about.

The series was born in discontent when Bobby Hull, the big winger who had jumped from the Chicago Black Hawks of the National Hockey League to Winnipeg of the World Hockey Association, was excluded from the Canadian team. Even Prime Minister Pierre Trudeau, acting behind the scenes, was unable to change the minds of the NHL executives. The Golden Jet was near tears when he was told. "Well then, it's the NHL against the Russians, not Canada," he said.

Thus, Team Canada was short two incredible Bobbys when they faced the Soviets. Bobby Orr is there in the team picture, but he didn't get into any of the games because of a ripped-up knee. He did travel with the team, and fans at each stop prayed that this would be the night the magical young Boston defenceman might crack the lineup.

Game One, Montreal, September 4, 1972: Esposito scored the first goal before the series was 30 seconds old. Paul Henderson made it 2–0 and it appeared that Espo's eight-straight prediction might be coming to pass.

Espo and Henderson—it was the combination that would haunt the Soviets all through the tournament but it didn't prevail this night. The visitors roared back and the final score was a stunning 7–3 victory for the Soviets. "It's a real competition now," coach Harry Sinden said.

Game Two, Toronto: Guess who scored the opening goal again? Right. It was Esposito, midway into the second period. Team Canada, with Phil's brother Tony in the net in place of Ken Dryden, allowed only one goal all night. Canada won 4–1 and the series was even.

Game Three, Winnipeg: This time Phil Esposito did not score the opening goal, but he assisted on it, feeding Jean-Paul Parisé with less than two minutes on the clock. The Canadians, however, blew a 4–2 lead as a result of two short-handed Soviet

goals, and ended up in a 4–4 tie after a scoreless third period. The series was tied tighter than ever.

Game Four, Vancouver: The last of the in-Canada games before the series adjourned to Moscow. Three times in the first period, Team Canada gave the Soviets a power play and twice the Soviets cashed in. Each time it was Boris Mikhailov on passes by Vladimir Lutchenko and Vladimir Petrov. Canada lost 5–3 and the fans booed the team off the ice.

Sinden, facing the journey to the U.S.S.R. down by a game, pointed at Vladislav Tretiak, who had turned back twenty-three shots in the third period alone, and said, "that guy was just exceptional—again."

Before Moscow, however, there were two exhibition games to play in Stockholm against the Swedish national club. Canada won 4–1 and tied 4–4 but both games were brutal. In the first game, Esposito got a 14-minute penalty—two minutes for cross-checking, two minutes for charging, and ten minutes for "yelling at the referee." In the second game, it was Bill Goldsworthy's turn —two minutes for cross-checking, two minutes for spearing, and an automatic ten minutes which goes along with a spearing call. After the game, Sinden shook his head over the officiating and co-coach John Ferguson said later, "what they called we deserved—but what they missed

was brutal."

Game Five, the first of the final four in Moscow: Everybody was on hand—Communist party General Secretary Leonid Brezhnev, Premier Alexei Kosygin and President Nikolai Podgorny. They saw Team Canada blast to a 3–0 lead going into the third period. And then the roof fell in. The Soviet leaders were out of their seats cheering as their team came back with five third-period goals to win 5–4. The Canadians were stunned. This series was supposed to have been a romp. Now they had to win all three of the remaining games.

Game Six was, if nothing else, different. All the scoring came in the

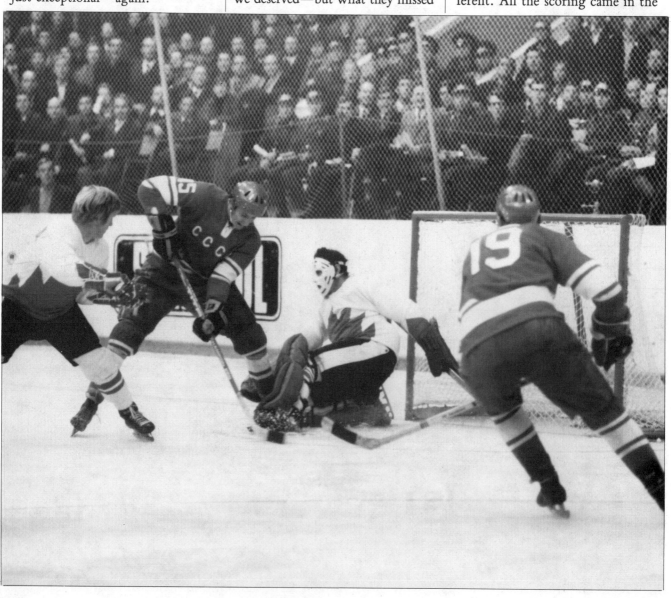

second period: Yuri Liapkin touching it off for the Soviets, and Canada answering with three goals—by Dennis Hull, Yvon Cournoyer and Henderson—within 90 seconds. Alexandre Yakushev got one back, but it was a case of too little, too late.

After the game, an international incident was almost touched off when Sinden, at a press conference, said the West German referees were "two of the worst officials I have ever seen handle a hockey game at any time of my career."

Game Seven: Once again it was Esposito who opened the scoring, just as, once again, it was Henderson who closed it. Henderson's goal on a pass from Serge Savard at 17:54 of the third period broke the tie to give Team Canada another one-goal victory, 4–3. It was the fifth time in seven games that the Toronto Maple Leafs' winger had been involved in Team Canada's final goal. He scored four of them and assisted on another.

The only statistic that really mattered, however, was the one showing the series all tied, 3–3–1. Now it was sudden death—one game for the championship.

Game Eight: There was a suggestion, for a time, that it might not happen. The problem? Go back to Game Six. Team Canada won it 3–2, then blasted the officiating by West Germans Josef Kompalla and Franz Baader. Canadian coaches Sinden and Ferguson, supported by their players, termed the Kompalla-Baader act "biased, incompetent refereeing." They pointed to one incident where Team Canada was called for icing— while a Canadian player was off serving a penalty. Canada picked up 31 minutes in penalties to four for the Soviets—in the second period alone.

The Canadians sought and received assurances from the Soviets that the West German pair would not be allowed to work another game. But in Game Eight, with the entire series on the line, the Soviets said it was all a misunderstanding. Kompalla and Baader would be in the striped shirts as originally called for under the rotation. "We might

as well quit right now," Esposito said. "We might as well give up and let the Russians have it if those guys work." Paul Henderson felt the same way: "I don't often get upset but the last game they worked, I nearly popped one of them."

The dispute ended in compromise. Each team got to pick one of the two officials. The Soviets, to nobody's surprise, picked Kompalla. Canada called for Rudolf Batja of Czechoslovakia. Even so, the game was delayed early in the first period by a dispute over a penalty call that resulted in the ejection of Parisé, the gutsy little left-winger for the Minnesota North Stars. Kompalla called an interference penalty against Parisé and when the player argued, he tacked on a ten-minute misconduct. A game misconduct followed when Parisé swung his stick at the West German.

The Soviets were leading 1–0 at the time, on a power-play goal by Yakushev, while Canada was two men short. It was beginning to look like a replay of Game Six. This time, however, the penalties were going both ways.

The teams traded power-play goals in the first period. Esposito put away Brad Park's rebound with Soviet defencemen Gennady Tsygankov off for interference. Vladimir Lutchenko drove home a screened shot from just inside the blue line while Cournoyer was serving a similar penalty.

With the teams at full strength, Park tied the score 2–2 on a pretty passing play with his New York Rangers teammate, Jean Ratelle. It didn't last long as a tie, though. The second period was only 21 seconds old when Ken Dryden, the hulking youngster they called "The Monster" in college, lost sight of the puck. It rebounded out to Soviet centre Vladimir Shadrin, who fired it past Dryden from 25 feet out.

Bill White, Chicago Black Hawks

defenceman, pulled Canada even once more when he tipped in a goal-mouth pass from the Rangers' Rod Gilbert. But it was Yakushev once again who, getting the puck from Shadrin on a face-off in the Canadian zone, made it 4–3 for the Soviets, barely a minute later. The U.S.S.R. went two up late in the second, on a goal credited to Valery Vasiliev, while the Black Hawk's Pat Stapleton was off for hooking. From the press seats, it appeared that Shadrin had tipped in Vasiliev's long shot.

Pete Mahovlich, the towering winger from the Montreal Canadiens, set up Esposito at 2:27 of the third period and the Bruin scored, even though it took him two belts, ramming home his own rebound. Cournoyer, the little Road Runner from Montreal, finally tied it at

12:56, off a rebound by Esposito on a play started by Park.

Esposito was playing like a man possessed. Sinden and Ferguson were screaming at him from the bench, trying to get him to come off for a rest. Possibly, Esposito didn't hear them in the uproar, but that's not likely. Sinden, at one point, had to be restrained from throwing something to get the burly centre's attention.

The teams went end to end. Espo dug the puck out of a pile-up at the side of the Soviet net but Tretiak stopped his shot. Henderson got the rebound and Tretiak stopped that. The score was 5–5 and time was running out. There would be no overtime. Henderson whacked at his own rebound and the score was 6–5 with only 34 seconds left on the clock. Team Canada had won.

If you were alive in Canada in 1972, you know how the country went nuts. Switchboard operators at Maple Leaf Gardens in Toronto were answering calls with "Maple Leaf Gardens—home of Paul Henderson . . ."

But if Canadians were high on victory, it was nothing to the elation in the Team Canada dressing room under the stands at the Luzhniki Ice Palace. "This is the happiest moment of my career," Henderson said. Dryden, unbuckling his heavy equipment, said, "this has to feel greater than winning the Stanley Cup," and Esposito agreed. "I was more emotional in this series than I ever was in the Stanley Cup," he said.

Esposito, who never let the Soviets forget how he felt about their system of government—"it stinks" —was something of a hero to the Russian hockey crowd. Coming out for introductions at the start of one game in Moscow, Espo performed a pirouette and fell flat on his hockey pants to the delight of the audience. When he appeared for introductions at the next game, Espo grinned, grabbed the boards in both hands and didn't let go until he was back in position. The Soviets loved it.

And it was Espo who touched off howls of hilarity in the dressing room when he tried to explain how the final goal came about. "I was behind the net and I saw Henderson flying in," he said. "I fired on the net and the rebound went to Paul and he put it away."

Then he was asked to detail his second goal which put Canada back in the game early in the third period. "Pete (Mahovlich) got the puck in the corner and flipped it out. I knocked it down with my hand right in front of the net. Then I juggled it a bit and slapped it in. After that, we got one more goal and won the whole thing 5–4. I remember every detail. I'll never forget that moment."

"No, Espo," a reporter said. "You didn't win it 5–4. You won it 6–5. There were two more goals scored." The big centre from Sault Ste. Marie, Ontario, looked shocked. "We did? Was that the score? Was that what happened?"

Below: Tretiak's brilliance took most Canadians by surprise

Parisé tried to explain how he came to be thrown out of the final game. "It was a good, honest check," he said. "Aleksandr Maltsev had the puck and I hit him. Then I got called for interference. You can't be called for interference when you're checking a man with the puck —crosschecking, charging, boarding, maybe, but not interference." It had been a tense moment. The Canadian bench threw a stool, then a metal chair on the ice. When Kompalla skated by, someone threw a towel at him.

There had been another tense moment, too, in that final game. Al Eagleson, player advocate and one of the organizers of the tournament, had his second encounter with Soviet police. Eagleson said he was en route to point out to the referee that the light had not gone on when Park scored his goal and "the next thing I knew I was on my way to Siberia."

In retrospect, it was hilarious. Team Canada players skated over to rescue The Eagle. Other players— including Gary Bergman—jumped over the boards. Bergman, however, landed astride and his fearful scream of anguish caused the Soviet police to wheel around. Eagleson scuttled to the safety of the Canadian bench, a perch from which he watched the remainder of the game.

After the series was over, Henderson sought out the young Tretiak, who was destined to go on to become one of the greatest goalies ever to play the game. "Tell him he played very well," Henderson said to the interpreter. After the relay, the interpreter turned back to Henderson. "He says you were lucky to score that goal." The veteran looked at the rookie for a long moment. "Tell him to go to hell," he said.

Right: Paul Henderson—THE GOAL!

Karen Magnussen

FROM SNOWFLAKE TO ICE QUEEN
BY GRANT KERR
THE CANADIAN PRESS, VANCOUVER

Karen Magnussen made her skating debut at age six, as a blond, blue-eyed snowflake in a winter carnival. Fourteen years later, she was crowned the world's figure skating queen in Bratislava, Czechoslovakia.

Magnussen's road to stardom wasn't without its icy detours, complete with stress fractures to both legs. But she proved to be champion material, refusing to become discouraged, even when she had to watch the 1969 World Championships from a wheelchair. "Even as I sat there, I was planning for next year's competition," she said later. "I never considered giving up; I always knew I'd be back."

On March 1, 1973, she became just the third Canadian to win the women's world singles title, following Barbara Ann Scott in 1947 and Petra Burka in 1965.

Two years after Magnussen began her skating career in the Vancouver winter carnival, she served notice that she might be something special when she won the B.C. Coast Championship in the novice division in 1961. The Magnussen household in North Vancouver was never really the same after that. Her parents, Gloria and Alf Magnussen, knew they had a champion in the making and made the personal sacrifices necessary for her development.

Magnussen's coaches played their parts too, from Dr. Helmet May to Eddie Rada, and finally Linda Brauckmann, who would be the steadying influence during the frustrating years when Magnussen couldn't beat Trixie Schuba of Austria. Magnussen, five times Canadian senior women's champion, finished second to Schuba in the 1972 Worlds in Calgary and in the Olympic Games the same winter in Sapporo, Japan.

But Magnussen was not going to be denied the ultimate prize in skating. She trained for ten hours a day in the summer and five to six hours daily in the winter, determined that 1973 would be the year she earned her just reward. Magnussen won her fifth Canadian senior title in Calgary, and then it was on to Bratislava for a showdown with American champion Janet Lynn.

Lynn and Magnussen had never quite been able to overcome Schuba, an unexciting but technically sound skater who always took a substantial lead in the compulsory figures and held on through the free skating routines favored by North Americans. But Schuba had retired and in 1973 it was Magnussen and Lynn who were poised to take advantage of a new marking system by the International Skating Association. The compulsory figures received 20 per cent of the final points total, with another 20 per cent for free skating exercises and 60 per cent for the exciting and entertaining free skating.

English journalist Clive James captured the moment in Bratislava when he wrote: "The spirit of the art was free to flourish and Magnussen turned in an absolute face-freezer—a display of power that ran like cold fury on silver rails."

Just thirty-four days before her twenty-first birthday and six years after her first appearance in the world championships, Karen Magnussen's flair for dazzling presentation in free skating brought her to the pinnacle of her sport.

The first Western Canadian figure skating champion later had an arena named in her honor in North Vancouver.

Karen Magnussen flanked by Janet Lynn (left) and Christine Errath

Turcotte and Secretariat

TRIUMPH AND TRAGEDY

BY CHRIS MORRIS

THE CANADIAN PRESS, FREDERICTON

It is a rare moment when time, place and the elements work together to produce a sporting legend. For Ron Turcotte, it happened while riding one of the greatest race horses in history—Secretariat.

A onetime lumberjack from a remote corner of New Brunswick—a province that doesn't even have a flat-racing track—Turcotte began his career as a jockey in Toronto in 1961. From there, he rode his way through the cutthroat world of thoroughbred racing to that supreme moment when he booted Secretariat home in the Belmont Stakes, 31 lengths ahead of the field.

With that victory on June 10, 1973, Turcotte and the big, handsome horse from Virginia won the Triple Crown. "The Triple Crown hadn't been won for twenty-five years but I can remember when we started out on Derby Day, I was confident," Turcotte recalls. "I knew Secretariat was the horse to break the jinx. He was the greatest horse I ever rode. He was really astonishing, and it's a great shame we never had a chance to see the true Secretariat, that he was retired before he reached his peak."

In his sixteen-month career, Secretariat won 17 of his 21 races before he was retired in October 1973, at the age of three, to a leisurely life standing at stud at a sprawling Kentucky farm. "His best year was still ahead of him," Turcotte says. "Riding Secretariat was like riding a Cadillac. But by his last two races, he had turned into a Rolls-Royce."

Below: Secretariat runs away from the pack at the Belmont Stakes

Turcotte's own career ended prematurely at Belmont Park in 1978. A fall from his mount shortly after leaving the gate shattered his backbone and left him paralysed from the chest down. He had been a jockey for seventeen years, winning 3,033 races and 29 million dollars in track purses. Known as the bettor's best friend, many thought that, like Secretariat, Turcotte's best years were still ahead of him.

Turcotte moved his family back to New Brunswick and built a beautiful stone house in Drummond, where, although confined to a wheelchair, he has become actively involved in community life and in several business ventures.

But the memories are hard to shake. "I get up some mornings and I really miss it," he once said. "Then, I try to chase it out of my mind and it doesn't bother me so much. But come Derby time, the Preakness and the Belmont, I watch the races on television and I wish I was there . . . it really gets in your blood."

Cindy Nicholas

THE DOUBLE CROSSING

BY BRUCE LEVETT

THE CANADIAN PRESS, TORONTO

"I beg your pardon, madam, but we seem to have a lousy connection here. I could have sworn you said 'ten hours' . . ." The telephone call from The Canadian Press in London to a cottage on the southern coast of England, was indeed crackling with static—but there had been no mistake.

Audrey Scott, secretary of the Channel Swimming Association, had just confirmed that Cindy Nicholas had not only swum the English Channel non-stop both ways, but had knocked an incredible ten hours five minutes off the record. And that was the men's record because, until Nicholas came along, no woman had accomplished the double crossing.

It was September 8, 1977, and Nicholas was a twenty-year-old Toronto student, destined—a few years off—to become a lawyer. But at that time, the Channel held a particular fascination for her, far beyond that of any other body of water she had challenged and conquered. When she slipped into the water off Shakespeare Beach that Wednesday, she was going for the England-to-France record—she had already set the record for the France-to-England swim in a previous attempt.

Nicholas went out in eight hours

Cindy Nicholas in action

58 minutes, and missed the record by two minutes. Then she turned around and swam back in ten hours 57 minutes—understandably nowhere near her own record of 9:46.

Her next major challenge to that filthy, storm-swept stretch—Nicholas once said it was like swimming through a sewer—came four years later when she went back to try for a triple crossing. It was something nobody, male or female, had ever done and Nicholas wanted to be the first.

She did accomplish another double, but weather forced her from the water short of her goal. A few days later, Jon Erikson, an American teacher, captured the triple crown she had wanted so badly. It was an ironic twist, for it was Erikson's record she had shattered so triumphantly in 1977—the two-way crossing that had made her queen of the Channel and resulted in her being voted Canada's female athlete of the year in the Canadian Press poll.

Crazy Canucks

FOR THE LOVE OF SPEED
BY MATTHEW FISHER
THE GLOBE AND MAIL

On Saturday, March 11, 1984, the last and the greatest of the five original Crazy Canucks retired. For almost a decade, Steve Podborski and his teammates, Jim Hunter, Dave Irwin, Dave Murray and Ken Read, had thrilled and perplexed alpine Europe. The articulate, well-groomed skiers from highly urbanized corners of the New World had shown they could compete against and beat Europe's storied mountain men at their own beloved game. Between December 1975 and January 1984, the Canadians won 14 World Cup downhills in Europe, including four consecutive victories at the supreme test, the Hahnenkamm at Kitzbuehel, Austria.

With the possible exception of Podborski, who skied with more grace and technique, the Canadians did it with a devil-may-care style that was much admired but seldom copied in Europe. Unlike many of the Europeans who often spoke in opaque and highly localized dialects, they enhanced their celebrity by being able to speak to the media in English, French and German. They had another advantage. In Europe, where the Swiss despised the Austrian racers and the Austrians reviled the Swiss, the Canadians were everyone's second most popular team.

At home, good press coverage was longer in coming. A nation educated to admire hockey and football players had some difficulty accepting Canadian ski stars. While twenty Canadian reporters attended the Super Bowl and hundreds took in the Stanley Cup finals, in the early days of success the Crazy Canucks were seldom watched by more than two or three.

The first Canadian to win was Read. In December 1975, the boyishly handsome nineteen-year-old upset the Austrians and Swiss in "The Test of the First Snow" at Val-d'Isère, France. Read's victory was a revelation. Until then, Canadian alpine success had always been a female prerogative. Canada's Sports Hall of Fame had already welcomed Anne Heggtveit, Lucille Wheeler and Nancy Greene, and would later admit Kathy Kreiner, the 1976 Olympic giant slalom winner. That the win at Val-d'Isère was not an aberration was established two weeks later when Irwin careered audaciously down the high-speed "Autobahn" at Schladming, Austria, with the fastest time.

The French journalist and World Cup founder Serge Lang was credited with labelling the newcomers as Crazy Canucks. In the early years it was an appropriate description, capturing their zest for the dangerous side of the sport. But for some reason, never explained, Lang spelled it "Cannucks" and that is how it was always printed in Europe.

The Crazy Canucks emerged from small ski clubs across the country. The first to gain entry into the favored top seed was "Jungle" Jim Hunter, a God-fearing Saskatchewanian who, perhaps because of the strength of his religious convictions, had trouble getting along with his teammates. But his skill and determination were an inspiration to

Right: Steve Podborski airborne at Whistler, B.C.

them. Although he would never win a race, he was one of the best in the mid-'70s. The next oldest was Murray, the laid-back son of a jumbo jet pilot from the flatlands of British Columbia's Fraser River delta. He was never a winner, either, but he came within hundredths of a second of victory twice and stayed in the middle of the first group for several years.

Only Irwin came close to the traditional alpine racing model. Like many of his European opponents, he grew up at his parents' ski resort. But the knoll on which he trained in bitter cold at Loch Lomond, near Thunder Bay, was a molehill compared with the impressive peaks which surround the warm chalets that house Austrian stars like Franz Klammer and Karl Schranz.

Read, who was to win five races and capture thousands of women's hearts, was a doctor's son from Calgary. He became famous for his windmill racing style and his work to make the World Cup competition safer and more professional. Read, whose victories included a rare back-to-back double at Kitzbuehel and Wengen, stayed in the first seed for a record eight consecutive seasons and just missed winning several World Cup titles in the late '70s. In 1979 his margin of defeat was only two-hundredths of a second.

Podborski was the youngest Crazy Canuck by a year and a half. He profited from his predecessors' mistakes and eventually became the most successful. When Read and Irwin won in 1975, Podborski was only eighteen but was already entering his

third season with the Canadian team. Growing up in the most unlikely of alpine communities, Toronto, he first tried skiing between his mother's legs on a little scrap of a hill beside the Don Valley.

The man who pulled the group together was Scott Henderson, a former racer from Banff, Alberta, who was highly regarded as a technical expert. From 1971 to 1977, at camps in Western Canada, the Alps and the Andes, the soft-spoken westerner taught his teenage students the virtue of hard work. At the same time he passed on his technical knowledge

Right: Crazy Canuck Dave Murray runs the slalom at Aspen, Colorado

Below: Ken Read

and encouraged them to follow their hearts. With the exception of Hunter, who also liked racing in slaloms and giant slaloms, the Crazy Canucks just wanted to go fast. Canada became the first country to concentrate exclusively on the downhill.

"The guys didn't know it but Jimmy (Hunter) was the guy who got them there," Henderson recalled. "They couldn't conceive of beating the world's best, but they could try to beat the guys they were with. The guys hated him. They wanted to beat him. He was the driving force. Kenny, a good glider but only a so-so turner, had the tenacity to get there. Irwin's problem was always gliding. He used too much hip. Because of this he couldn't do well on certain hills. I was sure Pod was going to be best

eventually because he had the talent. He was a good glider and a good turner."

"I remember Scott gave us the 'go for it' spirit," Podborski said. "It may sound funny now, but we went around telling each other to go for it. We believed it." Podborski got it right more often than any of his teammates. He conquered the field and the mountains eight times. He was first three times at Garmisch, West Germany, and twice at Kitzbuehel; won at Morzine, France, and St. Moritz and Crans Montana in Switzerland; was a bronze medallist at the Lake Placid Olympics in 1980; finished in the medals at World Cup races 25 times; and, between January 1980 and January 1984, had more top-three finishes than any other racer in the world. Best of all, in 1982,

he became the first non-European to win the World Cup downhill title.

"The most satisfying thing was winning the World Cup," Podborski said. "It wasn't like winning a race, where you could go 'wow' but it was the kind of accomplishment that could make you smile for a few minutes."

Podborski backed into his first World Cup victory at Morzine in December 1978. He had placed second to Read, who was disqualified for wearing an illegal downhill suit. In December 1980, it was Podborski's turn to be deprived of a victory although the circumstances were somewhat different. He led a downhill at Schladming by more than a second when it was called off because of rain after twenty-nine racers had made their run. If one more

skier had left the starting hut, the result would have counted and the winning points would have given Podborski the World Cup downhill title.

Along with success, pain was a constant companion. Podborski shredded his knees three times in skiing accidents, and each time the recovery took many months and thousands of hours of treatment. Each time he came back to win races. "The low points in my career were when I wrecked my knee," Podborski said. "The first time it happened I was devastated but making it through toughened me. I think it was the key point in my career. Here I was whipping down a hill, thinking I was in control, and I lost it. One minute it was me against the hill. Suddenly it was me, the doc-tors and the physiotherapists. It was a tough transition. Until then skiing had been fun. It helped me realize that to get it right you must make a huge commitment. If you don't and you get hurt again, you ask yourself if you've done enough."

Crashes also interfered with the careers of Read and Irwin. At Garmisch in 1981, Read went down near the finish line, his body rotat-ing around his knee as he decelerat-ed from 110 kilometres per hour. He returned for one more season and then retired. Irwin's injuries were harder to measure but even more debilitating. A few weeks after win-ning at Schladming, the strongest, wildest and most daring of the Cra-zy Canucks came to grief on a fallaway turn at Wengen, Switzer-land. He crashed through snowbanks and across ice and rock, battering his head badly. After a long, anxious moment on the hill, he was flown by helicopter to a hospital in nearby Interlaken where he lay in a coma for some hours. A year later, on the same course, he fell heavily again. Although he hung on for several more seasons, he never rediscovered the brazen form that took him to victory at Schladming. Before his head injuries, Irwin had been a good racer who had mastered the fine points which separated those with the "royal jelly" from others who were always half a second behind.

Winning required a special kind of memory. Racers had to learn the

Below: Dave Irwin in 1982
Right: Steve Podborski is hoisted up by Dave Murray (left), and Todd Brooker after winning the World Cup

mountains after only one or two inspection runs. As they whistled downhill at speeds of up to 140 kilometres per hour, they needed acute vision to spot potentially troublesome pot-holes or a small patch of glare ice. And they had to have an extra sense to gauge exactly when to tuck a little longer or a little lower to gain a few extra hundredths of a second. In the racers' own colorful argot, if these qualities temporarily eluded them they risked "doing a face plant" or "eating my liver." Life in the fast track required two minutes of skiing the thin line between first place and disaster. Read and Podborski called it "living on the edge."

But how did Canadians even get to the point where they could realistically contemplate life on the edge? Switzerland and Austria had more money and much larger development programs. Henderson obviously had something to do with the success of the Crazy Canucks, but the explanation is probably more complicated. Chance brought together five young men in the early 1970s. Each had the small, compact body that often does well in downhill. They loved the sensation of speed and were willing to take chances. They learned from each other and from their coach as if by osmosis. For a time they were among the best racers in the world, hogging the sports pages to present a view of Canada that was at variance with the ugly image Canadian hockey players had frequently presented to the Old World.

Despite their many triumphs, the Crazy Canucks left no legacy. There is no group of young Canadians qualified to replace them. Given the tiny

size of our talent pool when compared with alpine nations and a domestic ski industry that is much smaller than those of a dozen other countries, it is unlikely the Great White North will ever again produce five comparably brave and skilled young skiers at the same time. What will be remembered is that for a few years Canada challenged Europe at a game they had thought their own.

Right: Kathy Kreiner at Lake Placid

*Right: Podborski waves goodbye to fans at
    Whistler in 1984, following his final
    race*

Kathy Kreiner

A DREAM COME TRUE
BY IAN MACLAINE
THE CANADIAN PRESS, TORONTO

Her eyes gazed wistfully at the snow, peering only occasionally at the electronic scoreboard as skier after skier catapulted into the finish area. It was Friday the 13th, and Kathy Kreiner stood alone at the bottom of the women's giant slalom run at Axamar Lizum, a trendy ski resort area 30 kilometres up in the Austrian Alps, west of Innsbruck.

The shy, eighteen-year-old schoolgirl from Timmins, Ontario, was the first skier to complete her run and some 20,000 fanatic Europeans lined the course awaiting the arrival of their favorites in the contest for the 1976 Olympic title.

Everyone said West German Rosi Mittermaier was a shoo-in. She had already won the downhill and slalom and was looking for an unprecedented sweep of all three gold medals in women's skiing. The other two Canadians in the field, Kathy's sister, Laurie, and Betsy Clifford, were starting among the second and third seeds with no chance at the medals.

"Hey, it's not the greatest start number but it's not the worst," said Luc Dubois, head of the Canadian ski program, when Kathy drew the number 1 position. "If she gets a good line, she could win it all."

She got a good line. Her time over the 1,225-metre course with 49 gates and a vertical drop of 385 metres was a fast one minute 29.13 seconds. Now it was a question of what the rest of the field could do.

Jacot Michelle of France came through two and one-half seconds slower than Kreiner's time. Young Hanni Wenzel of Liechtenstein, a future champion, was nearly three seconds off the pace. Then Mittermaier, spurred on by a cacophony of "Hop! Hop! Hop!" from her compatriots lining the hill, slashed across the finish line. The West German's intermediate time had been the fastest and as she flashed under the finish banner, an interminable moment of silence enveloped the hill as all eyes shifted to the leader board.

The timer told the story—1:29.25 —twelve one-hundredths of a second slower than Kreiner. Mitter-

maier showed the class of a true champion by skiing over immediately to the lonely figure in the outrun and giving her a congratulatory embrace. Several of the world's top skiers were still on the hill—Daniele Debernard of France, Swiss aces Lise-Marie Morerod and Marie-Theres Nadig and Italian Claudia Geordani — but Mittermaier's gesture proved prophetic and launched a victory party by the Canadian skiers and coaches.

It was much, much later, after she had been joined by her sister and Clifford, that it finally got through to the blonde teenager that her dream had come true. She had won the gold and stolen the hearts of the European skiing community.

Right: Kreiner takes the gold

Villeneuve

DRIVING ON THE EDGE
BY GUY ROBILLARD
THE CANADIAN PRESS, MONTREAL

There was probably no Canadian of his generation who was as widely known abroad as Gilles Villeneuve. In Europe, Brazil, Argentina, South Africa, Japan and elsewhere on the globe, he was very big news, for Formula One auto racing is truly an international sport. Several hundred million people witnessed his Grand Prix races on television or saw highlights of his feats on televised sportscasts. The most spectacular driver of his time, he became a citizen of the world who lived in Monaco, trained in Italy and performed before millions all over the globe. Some 150 Gilles Villeneuve fan clubs remain in Italy where they

have not forgotten *Il Piccolo Canadese*. But, because Formula One is not a major sport in North America, the Villeneuve legend never flourished to the same extent in his native land.

A Canadian succeeding in Formula One as a member of the prestigious Ferrari team is a spectacular achievement in its own right. Thousands of young drivers from around the world have the same dream and much more advantageous conditions, but Villeneuve emerged from Quebec, where automotive sports have relatively little tradition. Added to all that is the fact that he started out without money and sponsorship

in a sport where the machines usually go to the richest, not the most talented.

On the credit side were those two great intangibles: talent and desire. A teenaged Gilles Villeneuve once confided to a friend that ''one day I'll be a Formula One driver.'' In Berthierville, Quebec, at the time, it was the equivalent of predicting he'd walk on the moon.

His father Seville understood his son's passion for speed and never discouraged either of his sons. Today, Jacques Villeneuve, like Gilles a former Canadian champion who has had tryouts in Formula One, is a regular on the Formula Indy circuit.

Gilles Villeneuve's love of speed also brought with it the inevitable risks. His first accident was an indication of things to come. The proud owner of a bicycle fitted with training wheels, he came to grief after he asked his father to remove

them so he could go faster. At age ten, he was riding one of the first ten-speed bikes ever seen in his home town and often "drove" the family sedan, sitting on his father's lap and imploring him to go faster. At fifteen, he wrecked the family car trying to take a curve at top speed in the rain. The car was a write-off but Gilles walked away, as he would in two subsequent accidents. His father was understanding: "I did just about the same thing at his age."

Young Villeneuve then bought and ran a series of clunkers that initiated him into the world of mechanics. While driving to Joliette to see Johanne, his future wife, he put on such a show of turning on two wheels in the tiny village of St. Thomas that people began asking when he would pass by again so they could line up to watch. He gravitated to stock-car racing on a dirt track behind a local hotel and the quarter-mile drags at Sanair. And then there were the "impromptu" competitions on area highways where the flagmen often were the local police. Winter weather was no hindrance in his quest for more speed — he simply traded in his car wheels for a snowmobile and became the world champion in snowmobile racing in 1974. He even built his own prototype which won many races for him.

His road career began in 1963 at age twenty-one and he quickly became Quebec champion in Formula Ford. After selling his house to finance his career, Villeneuve went on to become Canadian and North American champion in Formula Atlantic. In 1976 he won all of his Formula Atlantic races except one, in which he was leading when mechanical problems forced him to withdraw.

His Formula One debut the following year was spectacular. At the wheel of an outmoded McLaren in the British Grand Prix at Silverston, he qualified ninth on the starting grid, ahead of the factory's number 2 driver, Jochen Mass. During the race, he moved up to seventh after only nine laps but had to make an unplanned pit stop when his engine overheated. The problem fixed, he rejoined the race and finished eleventh.

He was named "driver of the day" and The Times wrote that "whoever seeks a future world champion need look no further than in the direction of this confident and quiet young man." And a reporter for France's prestigious sports daily, L'Equipe, wrote: "It is very rare that a newcomer makes the kind of impression created by Villeneuve." After the Silverstone race, Roberto Nosetto, bird dog for the elite Ferrari establishment, questioned French journalists: "Who exactly is this Villeneuve? Where does he come from? What language does he speak? Who did he race for before? Formula Atlantic . . . what is that?"

Villeneuve's adventure with McLaren came to an abrupt end when the sponsor, Marlboro, replaced him with Patrick Tambay. But, to the astonishment of many, Villeneuve was hired by Ferrari. Still a virtual stranger, the Quebec racer became one of the very rare drivers to make Formula One without European racing experience. Now, everyone was watching to see if he could take the pressure.

"He couldn't have found a better team with which to continue his Formula One racing career, but the pressure coming from the Italian media was terrible," says Niki Lauda, the world champion whom the Quebec driver was replacing. "And there wasn't only the media pressure, but that from the whole Ferrari team, which always had to win."

Below: Villeneuve celebrates a victory

While James Hunt, whom Villeneuve had beaten in Trois-Rivières' Can-Am race, was predicting that Villeneuve would win one of his first three Grand Prix races and could become world champion in his rookie year, Villeneuve maintained a very low profile. Despite difficulties which plagued his start, a crash at Mosport, Ontario, and a collision with Ronnie Peterson that drove him off the track and killed four spectators in Japan, Villeneuve still had the confidence of Enzo Ferrari for the 1978 season.

But the Quebecer got off to a slow start in the new season as well and Ferrari was openly second-guessed. Just as things were coming to a head, Villeneuve began showing his qualities, finishing nine of eleven races and finally chalking up his first win on home ground at the first Montreal Grand Prix. In 1979, he finished second in the World Championship for drivers, four scant points behind his teammate and Ferrari number 1 driver Jody Sheckter whom he often was forced to follow to the finish line in the spirit of team harmony.

It was Didier Pironi's refusal to play by the same rules that led to Villeneuve's death on May 8, 1982, at the very end of qualifications for the Belgian Grand Prix at Zolder. During the previous race at Imola, Villeneuve saw victory snatched away by his teammate, even though he was better placed in the drivers' standings.

The Berthierville Flash refused to accept this treatment and when Pironi once again surged ahead of him for a spot on the starting grid for the Belgian Grand Prix, an infuriated Villeneuve went back to the track for another qualifying run. On a straightaway, there was a mix-up in signals with Jochen Mass and Villeneuve tried to pass on the wrong side. The car crashed at more than 200 kilometres per hour, rolled over

several times, hit a wall, the seat came free, and Villeneuve died in hospital several hours later. Many observers felt it had only been a question of time. Appreciated for his aggressive and spectacular driving, Villeneuve already had walked away from too many crashes.

The race after Zolder took place in Monaco, where Villeneuve lived and where his wife and two children, Jacques, fourteen (a champion skier who dreams about a career in car racing), and Melanie, twelve, still live. The cover story of the official program, a moving tribute, was dedicated to him by Clay Regazzoni, a fellow-driver forced out of racing by injuries suffered at Long Beach, California.

"So long, Gilles," Regazzoni wrote. "You were young, loyal, daring, simple and you loved to express yourself in our sport like no one has done in recent years. You had just attained the heights of glory and like a lightning bolt, destiny cruelly stole your life. You leave an immense void. Your talents were fantastic exhibitions which the many fans you loved and for whom you always gave your best, will miss. They never will forget what you did, and you will leave unperishable memories for automotive sport aficionados. Johanne, Melanie and Jacques, like us, will always be proud of you. Adieu, Gilles."

Field Lacrosse

THE UPSET
BY NEIL STEVENS
THE CANADIAN PRESS, TORONTO

The Canadian team was not expected to do much when it arrived in Stockport, England, for the 1978 world field lacrosse championship. Nor did the weather do much to brighten the team's gloomy prospects. "We were there for sixteen days and it rained for fifteen-plus," recalls Stan Cockerton, who scored six goals during the game. "A light rain fell on and off during the championship game."

The United States had won the first three world championships, held every four years since being inaugurated in the mid-1960s, and had not lost a single game in international play before they met fourth-seeded Canada on that memorable day. Composed mainly of veteran box lacrosse players from Ontario and British Columbia, the Canadian team adjusted quickly to the larger playing area and different rules of the field game.

Tied 16–16 after the regulation four 25-minute straight-time quarters, Canada and the United States entered two four-minute overtime periods. Neither team could score in the first extra session, during which Canada killed two penalties. The minutes evaporated in the second overtime period until, with only one minute remaining, the U.S. side was penalized and Canada called a timeout.

Allan huddled with his players. On an earlier power play, Cockerton and Mike French had worked a play that had proved unsuccessful. Now they decided to give it another try. The plan was to overload one side of the field and send Cockerton down the other, breaking into the middle of the U.S. zone where

French would pass to him from behind the net. "I got the pass, faked a couple of times, waited until their goaltender went down and shot into the open top half of the net," Cockerton said. The winning goal came with 30 seconds left on the clock—too little time for the Americans to respond—and the Canadians took home the gold.

Below: Action at the championship

The Eskimos

EDMONTON'S DEVASTATING REIGN

BY JOHN KOROBANIK
THE CANADIAN PRESS, EDMONTON

"I want you to go out there and get me some first downs." Those were remarkably simple instructions from the brilliant and successful coach, Hugh Campbell, considering the situation. For it was midway through the second quarter of the 1981 Grey Cup game, and his heavily favored Edmonton Eskimos were trailing Ottawa Rough Riders 20–0 on a cold, miserable afternoon in Montreal's Olympic Stadium.

Campbell's words were directed at back-up quarterback Tom Wilkinson, nicknamed "The Little General," and one of the last of the Canadian Football League's great characters.

Using all the experience of his fifteen CFL seasons to do exactly what Campbell wanted, Wilkinson spread the Ottawa defence with a varied offensive attack. He ran Jim Germany left and right. He sent Neil Lumsden banging up the middle. He completed 10 of 13 passes by staying in the pocket when it held, and scrambling effectively when the Riders broke it down. He sacrificed himself for a team that prided itself on being a family.

Wilkinson played only ten minutes and put only one point on the scoreboard, on a wide Dave Cutler field goal. But he steadied the Eskimo offence and then gave a spirited half-time talk that rallied the team and inspired number 1 quarterback Warren Moon. Moon had suffered through the worst start in his magnificent CFL career, completing just one of nine passes and throwing two interceptions before Campbell sent in Wilkinson. But after seeing how effectively Wilkinson directed the offence, it was a different Moon playing in the second half.

Using all the skills that would later earn him a multi-million-dollar National Football League contract, the youngster from Los Angeles completed 12 of 18 passes and utilized a strong running game to rally the Eskimos for 25 points. Moon ran for two touchdowns himself, including one from two yards, midway through the final quarter, that capped a masterly 74-yard drive.

That made the score 23–21 and everyone, including the Ottawa defence, knew the Eskimos were gong for a two-point conversion. Moon rolled to his right and, with several Riders in hot pursuit, calmly fired the football to Marco Cyncar, cutting across the middle five yards into the end zone. With the score tied, middle linebacker Dan Kepley and the veteran Edmonton defence, which held Ottawa to just three points in the second half, throttled the Rider offence again.

Now the Eskimos had their chance to establish themselves as one of Canadian sport's all-time great dynasties. They clutched the opportunity with the unbreakable grip of a dying man. Reaching back to the experience of three consecutive Grey Cup championships, they resisted the temptation to strike quickly, and relied instead on patience. Four times, Germany, the often overworked and always underrated running back, kept the final, winning drive alive.

The ball was on the Ottawa 27-yard line and only three seconds remained on the clock when Cutler, the finest field-goal kicker in CFL history, stepped forth for his moment of glory. The snap from centre Bob Howes to Wilkinson was perfect and Cutler's attempt sailed through the uprights. "With Howes retiring, with Wilkie retiring, I thought it was destiny they would make that kick," Campbell said later.

The field goal gave Edmonton a 26–23 victory and their record-breaking fourth straight Grey Cup championship. The following year, without Wilkinson, the Eskimos won their fifth straight Grey Cup title. It was a farewell present to Campbell and also the end of Edmonton's era of excellence, the most devastating reign of any team in CFL history. During an unparalleled ten-year period, the Eskimos played in nine Grey Cup games and won six of them.

Right: Warren Moon lets one fly during the 1982 Grey Cup game

Below: Tom Wilkinson and Dan Kepley with the Grey Cup

Gaetan Boucher

THE WINNING HABIT
BY JIM PROUDFOOT
THE TORONTO STAR

For Gaetan Boucher, the greatest time of his life lasted less than six days, not even a week. It was long enough, though, for the boy from Ste-Foy, Quebec, to savor the sweet fruits of a decade's toil and a century's worth of dreams; long enough to conquer the agonizing spectre of self-doubt and to alter the course of a nation's sporting history.

The rewards for Boucher's years of effort began on February 10, 1984. The scene was the Olympic speed skating track on the site of an old cemetery in Sarajevo, Yugoslavia. Workmen, wielding brooms, battled a snowstorm to keep the ice clear. And then Boucher began to skate toward the fulfillment of a dream.

When the last event was won on the 16th, Gaetan Boucher had become Canada's most productive Olympian ever. Dominating the 14th Winter Games with his speed, he opened up with a bronze medal and followed that with triumphant, back-to-back golds. This haul, together with his silver from 1980, added up to a grand total of four medals—unmatched by any Canadian athlete since Canada first began attending the Olympic Games. Bou-

cher's achievements would lead to the psychological breakthrough which produced an unprecedented eleven victories for Canada at the Summer Games in Los Angeles. All of those California winners credited Boucher who had paved the way, set the tone, and shown them how to win.

"The ability to win is something very special," Boucher said in an inspirational talk to the team at Los Angeles. "You know, I was a very good skater for a long while before I got the knack of victory. I didn't believe, deep down, that I could be first. Only when that belief changed did those gold medals become possible. I went to Sarajevo expecting

Gaetan Boucher at Sarajevo

—not hoping—to win. It seems to me now that more and more Canadians are acquiring that same feeling. And if that is in some way a result of what I did at Sarajevo, it might be my greatest reward.''

Although a modest young man, Gaetan Boucher's self-confidence was unshakeable when he reached the Olympic site in the historic capital of Bosnia-Hercegovina. ''I have been skating very well this season,'' he pointed out. ''I have been defeating the people, particularly the Russians, who'll be my chief opponents here. I'll be disappointed, in fact, if I don't come away from Sarajevo with three medals. I can't say, though, what color they'll be.''

The 500 metres, definitely not Boucher's cup of tea, came first on February 10th. He placed third, a mere fifth of a second behind Sergei Fokichev of the Soviet Union. Afterwards, he was absolutely elated. ''I was never very good in the 500. Remember 1980 in Lake Placid? I was fourteenth and then I came second at 1,000 metres. Second to Eric Heiden, that is, which was as good as winning in a lot of ways.'' Heiden, the U.S. phenomenon, had gone on to an unprecedented gold-medal sweep in the speed skating events at Lake Placid.

In truth, as Boucher now admits, he made up his mind after his 500 bronze at Sarajevo that he couldn't possibly lose his next race. Nor did he. Competing on St. Valentine's Day, he defeated Soviet skater Sergei Khlebnikov by more than four-fifths of a second, a comfortable margin. ''At that point,'' he would say later, ''I could see that it was now possible for me to win the 1,500 as well. It is basically the same race, if you can somehow overcome the pain and fatigue through the final 300 metres.''

This time, on February 16, Khlebnikov ended up half a second behind Boucher. ''I have to tell you I was fortunate in the draw,'' Boucher observed. ''I was in the eighth pair to skate, which meant the ice was cleared just before I started. Also, Khlebnikov had gone before me so I knew exactly what time I had to shoot for.'' And so, on a bitterly cold evening in Sarajevo's main square, the Canadian flag was raised for the second time and Gaetan Boucher proudly accepted his second gold medal.

Below: Boucher rounds a corner in the gold medal winning 500 metre sprint
Right: Boucher (left) at age eleven

There had been so many times when he questioned whether such a moment would ever be his to enjoy. And these were doubts shared by many people who are knowledgeable about the sport of speed skating. There is Boucher's build, for one thing. "I'm too small. My body is not ideal for speed skating. I'm five-foot-nine. If you want to see the right size, look at Khlebnikov as an example. He's about six feet tall. That's perfect because it gives him a nice, long stride. Mine is short by comparison. I have to work a lot harder just to cover the same distance in comparable time." Dr. Bob Hindmarch, Canada's *chef de mission* at Sarajevo, had an answer for that. "The statistics don't say anything about the size of Gaetan's heart," he pointed out, "or his dedication in developing great technique."

A more serious problem was Boucher's own attitude and how it evolved over the years from the time he arrived on the international speed skating scene in 1975. He was, in fact, the classic Canadian loser. "I'd like to believe I didn't choke in those days but maybe I did," he said in retrospect. "It seemed I would often skate badly in the biggest contests. I can remember having the best time of anybody going into the world championships, and finishing fourth. Another year I lost a world title by a tenth of a second after skating a poor race technically. That's choking, I suppose.

"My reputation was that I'd always panic in an important situation. I was fine when I had perfect conditions and the opposition was weak but I seemed to lack toughness for real competition. I'm not sure, but I do know that's how the speed skating world saw me.

"I've changed. Some things just come to you with experience, of course. I got a lot of it from the people around me in skating and also from my family. Especially my family, I would say. They kept asking me what I was afraid of when I was one of the best. So a day came when I told myself that, hey, I really was one of the best, as they kept telling me. And finally, I believed it myself."

But there was to be another pitfall on the road to Sarajevo. In March of 1983, less than a year before the Olympics, Boucher was taking part in an indoor meet in Montreal and lost his balance while negotiating one of the cramped turns. He crashed into the hockey boards and broke an ankle. "For two days, the doctors didn't know if they could fix it or not—whether I'd ever be able to skate again," Boucher recalled. "I was a very worried guy. But it was a useful period, you know.

"I can remember looking at my foot turned in such an unnatural way and thinking the Olympics were gone for sure. So for the first time, I realized how much the Olympics meant to me. That accident gave me a perspective I'd never had before. Anyway, the operation was completely successful and I knew I would be as good as ever."

Eight weeks of recovery were required and that, too, proved beneficial. "It was a two-month break which I needed a lot more than I thought, after doing nothing but skate for such a long time," said Boucher. "I was tired, mentally and physically, and didn't even know it. When I began training again in the

fall, I was a new person. I came back to skating very refreshed and full of determination and I think the injury was really what did it."

Boucher was born in Ste-Foy, a suburb of Quebec City, and learned to skate on a tiny outdoor rink behind the hockey arena. His family lives outside Montreal now, in St-Hubert, which he lists as his home. In fact, though, as an international athlete, he is on the road most of the year and is, in a very real sense, a citizen of the world.

"I think I could have been a hockey player," he says, reflecting on his boyhood. "I was always a good skater, of course, and that is the most important thing. But I gave it up in 1975, when I made the national speed skating team for the first time.

"Sometimes it strikes me that in hockey I might have become a very rich guy, but even so, I'll always feel I made the right choice. I doubt that any hockey player has ever had the kind of feeling I experienced in Sarajevo during those days of the Olympics. I wouldn't trade it for anything."

Boucher expected the glory to end and the attention to evaporate when he walked away from the podium in Sarajevo. It hadn't occurred to him that he had become a celebrity. "Canadians don't care about speed skating," he argued. "Back home, when I tell people I'm an athlete from Quebec, they ask me if I play for the Nordiques or the Canadiens. I'm not upset about this. I've been in speed skating a long time. That's just the way things are. I'm used to it."

So the sequels to the Boucher saga came as delightful surprises. He was honored from coast to coast. He had to hire an agent to sort out the demands on his time and the commercial opportunities that came his way. His face got to be known on television. Much to his astonishment, he even made a bit of money.

Casual sports fans, mildly im-

pressed by his Olympic accomplishments, were bowled over when he proceeded to capture the world sprinting championship in Norway. He was certified then as a truly important performer, the genuine article. He did it in noteworthy fashion, too. Going into the final race, at 1,000 metres, he needed to surpass his old adversary Khlebnikov by at least .46 of a second to claim first place overall. In the sort of clutch effort that brings spectators to their feet in any stadium anywhere in the world, he eked out a .49 edge at the finish.

At a garden party in Beverly Hills, as the Los Angeles Games were getting under way, Boucher, who had been flown in to address the gathering of Canadian competitors and officials, summed up what winning was all about. ''For the first time I'm seeing a lot of Canadian athletes who don't have those traditional feelings of inferiority,'' he said. ''You know what I'm talking about. I do. I used to have them myself.''

''You'd go to the Olympics just hoping to finish in the top six or survive the preliminary round or whatever. We didn't seem to understand it but we were always preparing to lose—beaten before we even started. I was expecting to win in Sarajevo last winter. It wasn't a question of hoping. I wouldn't have been satisfied with second place. I was there to win. I detect the same thing here. We've got a lot of people who have come to L.A. to get gold medals, nothing less. And feeling that way, they'll succeed.''

In the days that followed, Alex Baumann, Victor Davis, Larry Cain, Anne Ottenbrite, Linda Thom, Sylvie Bernier and all the others did place number 1, and there were even some triumphs no one had anticipated. Such is the result of Boucher's achievement; everybody gets the hang of it and, suddenly, all the Canucks become hard to handle. Winning turns into a habit.

Preceding page: Boucher strikes gold

Below: A charging Boucher

1984 Olympics

CANADA'S GOLDEN SUMMER

BY MARK HARDING
THE CANADIAN PRESS, TORONTO

Gold medals and a glittering array of unforgettable performances are the legacy shared by Canadians, both those at home who watched on TV and those who went to southern California to watch or participate in the events of the Summer of '84. After 52 years, the eyes of the sporting world refocused on sun-baked Los Angeles for the Games of the 23rd Olympiad. It began on July 28 and ended on August 12, a sixteen-day extravaganza that will be remembered as Canada's finest performance at the Olympics.

When athletes representing thirty-seven countries last competed in an L.A. Olympics in 1932 on the then-revolutionary crushed peat track at the 100,000-seat Memorial Coliseum and surrounding venues, the Canadian medal haul consisted of two gold, five silver and nine bronze. Duncan McNaughton and Horace (Lefty) Gwynne were the heroes of the day, beating the world's finest for the men's high jump and bantamweight boxing titles. McNaughton, Gwynne and their teammates won 15 medals, an achievement unmatched by Canadian Olympians until the 1984 team returned to the scene of their triumph and carried off 44.

Because of the unfortunate Soviet-led boycott by eastern bloc countries, Canadian hopes for a record-shattering medal total had been buoyed. But the performances of the country's swimmers, divers, canoeists, rowers, yachtsmen, track and field stars, boxers, wrestlers, judoists, cyclists, gymnasts, weightlifters and shooters exceeded even the highest expectations of team officials.

The outstanding Candian per-

former at the Games was the first of the record 489-member contingent to enter the Coliseum on that sunny Saturday afternoon of July 28. Swimmer Alex Baumann of Sudbury, Ontario, a native Czechoslovakian who came to Canada at the

age of four, carried much more than the Canadian flag into the opening ceremonies. He was saddled with tremendous pressure. As a world record holder, new standards were expected of him. Winning would not be enough.

The setting for the twenty-year-old Baumann's heroics was the University of Southern California pool, where he was to defend his number 1 world ranking in the 200- and 400-metre individual medley. On Monday morning, July 30, he strode

confidently from the athletes' warm-up area at poolside to the starting blocks for his preliminary heat in the 400. Four minutes and 22.46 seconds after the starter's gun had fired, Baumann touched the pool's east wall to establish an Olympic record.

Could his tender shoulder stand up to another eight pool lengths of butterfly, backstroke, breaststroke and freestyle against seven other world-class swimmers less than eight hours later? This and other pre-race questions were answered at approximately 7:30 p.m. that Monday when Baumann outstroked Brazilian Ricardo Prado in the world-record time of 4:17.41. The young Canadian looked at the results board, and lifted himself straight out of the water with fists clenched in victory. Canada's 72-year thirst for gold in Olympic pools from Antwerp to Athens and Melbourne to Montreal had finally been quenched.

"It's been a long grind for Canada, but I'm glad we've finally struck gold again," said Baumann, who sports a tiny red maple leaf tattoo on his left breast. "I've worked a long time for this and I'm very proud to be a Canadian." As the strains of "O Canada" blared through a wall of speakers after the medal presentations and the Maple Leaf was hoisted to the top of the tallest flagpole, Baumann squinted into the setting sun. The tone had been set. One down, the 200 individual medley still to go.

Inspired by Baumann and an opening-day victory by pistol shooter Linda Thom of Ottawa, Canadian athletes assaulted the waters, tracks and rings of competition in the days that followed. They climbed the medal platforms with unprecedented

regularity and the Canadian identity crisis seemed to fade with every first-, second- and third-place finish.

As the pulse of the Games quickened, the spotlight returned to Baumann five days after his opening race. The questions began to resurface. Could he annihilate the opposition in the 200 individual medley as he had done in the 400? In the early-morning smog that enveloped the City of Angels on August 4, no fewer than eleven swimmers shattered the 14-year-old Olympic record of 2:07.17 during preliminary heats. And at the top of the heap was Baumann in a time of 2:03.60, approximately one second slower than his world mark of 2:02.25.

Several hours later, in one of the grittiest performances in Olympic history, Baumann became the first

Canadian swimmer to capture two gold medals since George Hodgson won two freestyle events at the 1912 Games at Stockholm. Not only did Baumann demolish the Olympic mark he set during his qualifying race, he gave swimmers a world-record time of 2:01.42 to shoot for and established himself as the finest all-round swimmer in the world. "I don't know if I'm the best in the world," Baumann said later. "I just set personal goals for myself and let the others decide whether I am the best in the world or not."

But Canada's success at the Olympic pool wasn't limited to Baumann. The other swimmers who helped the country land ten of its 44 medals were led by breaststrokers Victor Davis of Waterloo and fellow-Ontarian Anne Ottenbrite of Whitby.

Left: Alex Baumann greets Canadian fans in Los Angeles

Right: Anne Ottenbrite shows her winning form

Davis, another world-record holder, was mentioned in the same breath as Baumann prior to the Games when chances of striking gold were discussed and hyped. For several years, the two had enjoyed a friendly rivalry, always heaping praise on each other for their respective accomplishments.

Despite his prowess in the pool, Davis had achieved some notoriety for an incident at the 1982 Commonwealth Games at Brisbane, Australia. Enraged by the disqualification of the winning Canadian 4 × 100 medley relay team for a premature start, in the presence of the Queen, Davis kicked a deck chair and stormed out of the pool area sending towels, plants and a trash bin flying, amid a string of obscenities. Anyone who knew or understood Davis's intensity and will to win might have expected it, but he drew the anger of the media and public alike. Davis believed that he, the rest of the team and his country had been unjustly penalized. He had been denied a chance to be part of a gold-medal performance in an international field. Those who sought, or expected, an apology could forget it.

He was tagged a Bad Boy and the reputation still haunted him as he headed to Los Angeles to compete in the 100- and 200- metre breaststroke. His initial opportunity came on the first full day of swim competition in the 100 metres. After preliminary morning heats, the final shaped up as a showdown between Davis and Steve Lundquist of the United States, competing in his own backyard with thousands of spectators poised to cheer him on to victory.

It was a tailor-made situation for the feisty Canadian—to stick it to the favorite, right in his own pool. On this night, however, Davis was relegated to a silver medal. He touched home in world-record time, but was a scant 34 one-hundredths of a second behind Lundquist. For Davis, it might just as well have been 34 minutes. He repeatedly punched the water in frustration. Emerging from the USC pool, he took several strides and plunged headlong into the diving tank which also served as the swim-down pool. Davis stayed underwater for almost an entire pool length, alone with his thoughts and where he couldn't hear the deafening ovation accorded Lundquist. "I swam the race I wanted to swim," Davis said during a post-race interview. "Steve just swam faster." One could tell he was mustering every ounce of sportsmanship in his muscular frame. It was also obvious that he was already preparing himself for the 200-metre breaststroke four days later.

Below: Victor Davis churns through the water in the 200 metre breaststroke

In the 200, Davis was the reigning world record holder with a time of 2:14.58. He knew a similar clocking would be required for a gold medal, his only serious remaining shot at Olympic success. Leaving his adversaries gasping in his wake that Thursday night, Davis churned through the USC waters in a blistering 2:13.34 and a new world record. It was almost two full seconds quicker than the previous Olympic mark set by Briton David Wilkie at the 1976 Montreal Games. The silver medalist, Glen Beringen of Australia, was outside Wilkie's mark at 2:15.79. With his treasured gold medal dangling around his neck, Davis said afterwards that he wanted to be remembered as a "hungry young Canadian athlete, not a caveman."

Ann Ottenbrite duplicated Davis's feat, winning the gold in the 200-metre breaststroke and the silver in the 100. Unlike Davis, however, she had only been billed as a possible bronze medallist at best in both events. In the 200, she became the first Canadian woman to capture a swimming gold medal since the modern Summer Games began in Athens in 1896. Her victory came less than 15 minutes after Baumann's first gold-medal swim and she said later that her teammate's performance had been an inspiration. "When I heard the anthem, I felt so good for Alex," said Ottenbrite. "It was a tremendous boost for me."

Because she was not known as a proficient sprinter, Ottenbrite's silver-medal effort in the 100-metre breaststroke was perhaps even more surprising than her victory in the 200. But she wasn't finished yet. There was still the women's 4 × 100 medley relay. Ottenbrite swam the breaststroke leg of that event and teamed with Reema Abdo of Belleville, Ontario, Michelle MacPherson of Toronto and Pamela Rai of Delta, British Colum-

bia, to win a bronze medal, thus becoming the first Canadian Olympic swimmer with a complete set of medals in Olympic competition.

But the 1984 Summer Games didn't belong solely to swimmers. Diver Sylvie Bernier of Ste-Foy, Quebec, won the women's three-metre springboard competition (and the hearts of Canadians at home watching on TV), and Lori Fung of Vancouver was the first Olympic champion in rhythmic gymnastics. The men's rowing eight captured a

gold in a major surprise, while in canoeing Larry Cain of Oakville, Ontario, took the 500-metre Canadian singles title, and Hugh Fraser and Alwyn Morris the 1,000-metre kayak pairs.

In other events Canada came home with many silver and bronze medals. It was a time for Canadians that not even time itself will be able to dim.

Below: Gold medalist Linda Thom carries the flag at the closing ceremonies in Los Angeles

Gretzky

NUMBER 99

BY DICK BEDDOES

CHCH, TV 11

Some Saturday night in the Big Arena in the Sky, Wayne Gretzky will win a faceoff from Frank Boucher, beat Bobby Hull to the loose puck, dodge away from Eddie Shore's crunching bodycheck, elude Doug Harvey behind the net and tap in his own rebound off Georges Vezina's goal stick. And somewhere in the stands, a fan munching his ambrosiaburger will mutter: "How lucky can a guy get?"

It is the Canadian dream to become a hockey star, bringing strangers together in happy bondage and endless debate. Younger fans, unburdened with memories of Cyclone Taylor, Howie Morenz and Rocket Richard, have no trouble accepting the myth that Wayne Gretzky was born in a manger in Brantford, Ontario, and became a hockey deity. But the legend has no appeal to others, whose arthritic bones and shortening breath remind them that they are no longer young and who resent Gretzky for overtaking their contemporaries.

The big numbers in the National Hockey League belong to Gordie Howe—26 NHL seasons, 801 goals, 1,049 assists, 1,850 points. No one is remotely close to those career figures, yet. But in six years, Gretzky has had 429 goals, 693 assists and 1,122 points. If the Edmonton Oilers' phenomenon stays healthy and maintains his scoring average of .915 goals a game, he will reach 801 late in the 1989–90 season.

Two prominent non-participants in the Gretzky-Howe debate are Gretzky and Howe. "Because of Gordie I always wanted to play in Detroit," Gretzky told an interviewer. "When I got an NHL jersey, I knew it wouldn't be quite right if I wore number 9, so I settled for 99."

"Wayne is the greatest," Howe said when he presented Gretzky with his sixth Hart Trophy as the league's most valuable player. On another occasion, responding to my suggestion that the slightly built Edmonton centre would not have survived the hammering Howe took and handed out during his career, Howe's reply was crisp and definitive: "Wayne has the talent to have been a star in any era."

Gretzky's hockey began in Brantford, a hard-times town 105 kilometres southwest of Toronto. His father, Walter, was a bush-league player of modest distinction. Walter works for Bell Canada as a teletype repairman but his avocation was coaching Wayne. Walter flooded his yard to make a Gretzky arena where his eldest son could practise and taught him the fundamentals, the fancy moves to trick opponents.

Below: A familiar sight—Gretzky behind the net

Right: Gretzky scores against Finland

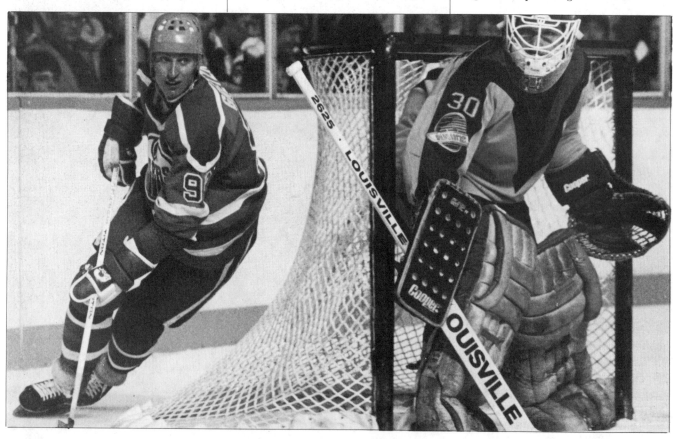

"Dad didn't force me," Wayne says. "It was what I wanted to do." At five, he was playing against kids who were ten. At eleven, he scored 378 goals in 85 games.

Walter made sure his son was different in other ways, too. One year, during a peewee tournament in Quebec City, Wayne wore glistening white gloves. As a pro, he still dresses distinctively. When he played with older children, he had to tuck his jersey into his hockey pants to avoid stepping on the hem. He no longer wears oversize equipment, but the right side of jersey number 99 is still tucked under his pants.

In 1977, the sixteen-year-old centre was playing major junior hockey, a step removed from the pros, with the Sault Ste. Marie Greyhounds. He was the good-luck charm on a team in a lunch-bucket Northern Ontario town where there are few illusions. But he soon began making locals forget two local boys who rose to remarkable prominence in the NHL—Phil and Tony Esposito.

Gretzky finished second in scoring in the Ontario Hockey League. His dazzle reminded some critics of another under-age OHL prodigy, Bobby Orr, who rewrote the book on playing defence and dominated two Stanley Cup victories by Boston Bruins before chronic knee problems ended his career at age twenty-eight.

Gretzky was a prize in the price war between the NHL and the World Hockey Association in the late '70s. Nelson Skalbania, a high-rolling sodbuster from Saskatchewan who owned the Indianapolis Racers of the WHA, signed him to a seven-year personal services contract. Walter Gretzky, aware that the Racers were playing to crowds so small that they considered it a big night when the other team showed up, insisted on an escape hatch that guaranteed Wayne $1.75 million if the team folded.

The Racers did fold after Gretzky played only eight games for them. Skalbania, trying to stay financially afloat, sold the contract to Peter Pocklington of the Edmonton Oilers. Pocklington, another high-roller who made and lost several fortunes on the volatile real estate market, extended the personal services contract to twenty-one years and pays Gretzky about one million dollars a year.

The NHL guides contain all the necessary facts, but none of the essential flavor of Gretzky. "How come nobody ever hits him?" I once asked Scotty Bowman of Buffalo Sabres, one of the smartest executives in the league. "It is almost impossible," Bowman said, "to hit a moonbeam."

He is a fluid, deceptive skater, faster than he looks. Let him sail across your blueline with two or three swift teammates and he'll turn your defencemen tanglefooted. He passes the puck with laser accuracy but softly, always seeming to target a Jarri Kurri or Paul Coffey on the fly. Only a team blessed with resolute forecheckers can disrupt the attack and few are capable of shutting it down consistently.

He is slim, a half inch under six feet, 175 pounds, his fair hair unruly at the fringes. He has a good, wide smile that you could stick a banana in. And he handles his accomplishments with grace.

"Will you keep cruising along and play as long as Howe?" I asked him that day before the Oilers won their second consecutive Stanley Cup.

"Oh, I won't play as long as Gordie. I'm not looking at records or years, but maybe after five more years I'll think that's enough."

"That might not be enough to break Howe's records," I said.

"I'd feel good," he said, "being number 2 to Gordie's number 1."

Rick Hansen

A MAN IN MOTION

BY AL SOKOL
THE TORONTO STAR

Rick Hansen, 28, will be remembered for a 25,000-mile wheelchair tour round the world, a trip through six continents and 34 countries, ending back in Vancouver in October 1986.

The first disabled person to graduate from physical education at the University of British Columbia, Hansen will also be remembered for a much shorter trip, 26.2 miles in the 1983 Toronto Marathon.

Hansen, whose legs were crushed in a truck accident thirteen years ago, won the wheelchair division of the '83 Toronto Marathon in two hours five minutes 20 seconds (2:05.20). That time is well under the world marathon running record of 2:07.11, set in 1985 by Portugal's Carlos Lopes, winner of the 1984 Olympic Games marathon, but well above Hansen's former world wheelchair mark of 1:58.17, set in 1982.

What made Hansen's Toronto victory so memorable was the sight of this remarkable athlete in the finish area of Varsity Stadium. His face was scraped and bloodied, not the type of injuries one usually associates with marathons. It turns out that at about the 10-mile mark Hansen got one of his wheels caught in a streetcar track on a downhill grade and was thrown from his chair. He and the wheelchair parted company and Hansen landed on his shoulder and face.

At this point Hansen, far ahead of the front runner, was obliged to retrieve his chair and get into it without any help from concerned bystanders. Any other athlete would probably have called it a day—a bad day—and waited for transportation back to Varsity Stadium. Instead, Hansen continued the race, blood streaming down his face and his shoulder aching.

''I never thought for a split second about quitting,'' explained Hansen at the finish line. ''I was more embarrassed than hurt. What bothered me more than anything else is the time I lost when I got thrown from the wheelchair. I knew I would finish. The point was I wanted to finish first.''

Hansen is definitely a winner. At the 1982 Pan-American Wheelchair Games in Halifax he won nine gold medals, competing in events from

Below: Rick Hansen—determination personified

100 to 1,500 metres and setting six world records in the process.

While the Edmonton Oilers' Wayne Gretzky won the '82 Lou Marsh Trophy, presented annually to Canada's top athlete—amateur or pro—the selectors singled out Hansen for the first Lou Marsh merit award.

In 1984 Hansen excelled in the Paralympics in England and made history by competing at the Olympic Games in Los Angeles that August in a special 1,500-metre race.

Hansen's Man in Motion World Tour set a goal of raising $10 million for spinal cord research, rehabilitation and wheelchair sports, as well as creating an awareness of the potential of disabled persons.

"Since the time of my accident, two major dreams have inspired me," recalled Hansen. "One is to help those people with spinal injuries and the other is to wheel around the world."

Hansen, of course, found a way to do both.

"Les Glorieux"

BY GUY ROBILLARD
THE CANADIAN PRESS, MONTREAL

To Quebecers, they are simply "les Glorieux."

In the seventy-five years since the Montreal Canadiens were founded in 1910, they have won 22 Stanley Cups, establishing a dynasty of excellence that surpasses even that of baseball's New York Yankees and basketball's Boston Celtics.

The Quebec people's identification with the team and the strength that characterizes it constitutes a unique loyalty that has scarcely waivered, even after Le Nordiques of Quebec City joined the National Hockey League as a latter-day rival.

Le Club de hockey canadien celebrated its 75th anniversary in 1984–85. During this period, 18 of its 22 Stanley Cups have come in the glory years that began with the 1943–44 season.

Under the benevolent dictatorship of Toe Blake, they won the Cup five consecutive years, a record that stands today, from 1955–56 through 1959–60. The team won four times in the '60s and closed out the '70s with four straight from 1975–76 through 1978–79, the latter under the guidance of William (Scotty) Bowman.

And even those statistics do less than justice to the juggernaut that has thrived in the legendary Forum at Atwater and St. Catherine streets in west-end Montreal. Over a three-year period from 1975–76 to 1977–78, for example, the Canadiens lost a mere 29 regular-season games, losing only eight of 80 games in 1976–77.

More importantly, when they didn't win Lord Stanley's silverware, they still iced formidable teams. Since 1947–48, the team has missed the playoffs only once, tying New York

Rangers for fourth place and losing out on the goal aggregate after being in the running for first place until the last weekend of play.

Since 1948, the Canadiens have finished fourth once (in 1983–84) and third in the league or their division five times. In the other 29 seasons, they were first or second.

A dwindling group of old-timers remains faithful to the memory of the team's earlier heroes—Georges Vezina, Newsy Lalonde, Howie Morenz, Aurel Joliat—but there is one name that inspires instant response from Canadien fans of every generation, that of Maurice (Rocket) Richard (1942–60).

Of course, The Rocket did not do it alone. He was the fiery triggerman of the illustrious Punch Line, centred by Elmer Lach and with Blake, later Bert Olmstead, on the

Beliveau and Geoffrion

The 1944 Canadiens—Stanley Cup champions

Three eras of the Montreal Canadiens are represented by Jean Beliveau ('50s and '60s), Guy Lafleur (1970s), and Rocket Richard ('40s and '50s)

other wing. The goaltender, Bill Durnan, was a perennial all-star, as were defencemen Ken Reardon and Emile (Butch) Bouchard.

Later, it would be the turn of Henri Richard, Jacques Plante, Doug Harvey, Bernard Geoffrion, Dickie Moore, Yvon Cournoyer, Frank Mahovlich and Jean Beliveau, the Rocket's successor in the hearts of fans, who would later pass the torch to Guy Lafleur. The latter would hold it high, with the help of Ken Dryden, Jacques Lemaire, Guy Lapointe, Serge Savard, Steve Shutt, Bob Gainey and Larry Robinson, the last survivors of the great epoch.

Of all of these names, that of Maurice Richard remains the most fabled. Whenever he is introduced to the public, he becomes the object of moving standing ovations, even from spectators who never saw him play.

During a recent fan poll to determine the Canadiens all-time team, he easily outdistanced Lafleur at right wing. The old-timers carried the day as Plante edged out Dryden in goal and Beliveau and Moore rounded out the starting forward line. The only Hab of recent vintage to break into the super six was Robinson, who joined the magical Harvey on the blueline.

At a recent NHL meeting, the league decreed that teams would play at full strength when coincidental minor penalties were assessed to both sides because some teams complained that the Edmonton Oilers were too effective in four-on-four situations. There is a precedent for the move.

In the league's first forty years, every minor penalty meant two full minutes in the penalty box. Then along came the devastating power play of Beliveau at centre, Maurice Richard on right wing, either Olmstead or Moore on left wing and Harvey and Geoffrion on the points. The Canadiens attack was so strong

Gordie Howe finds himself surrounded by Canadiens in 1957

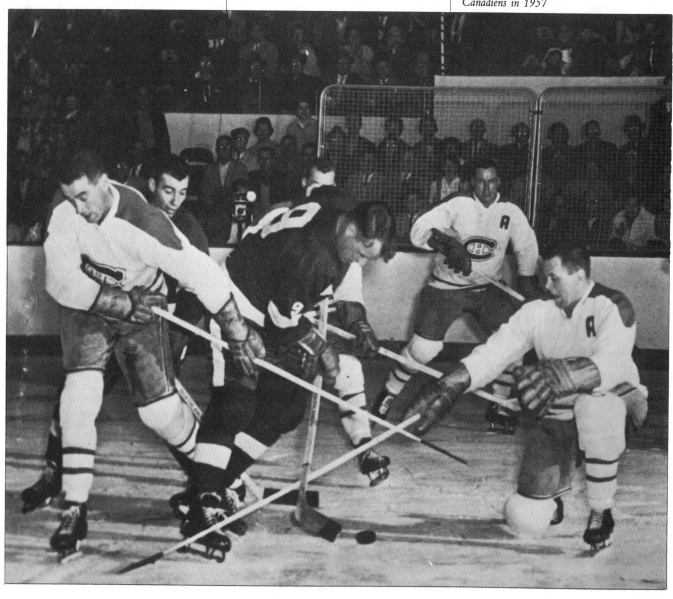

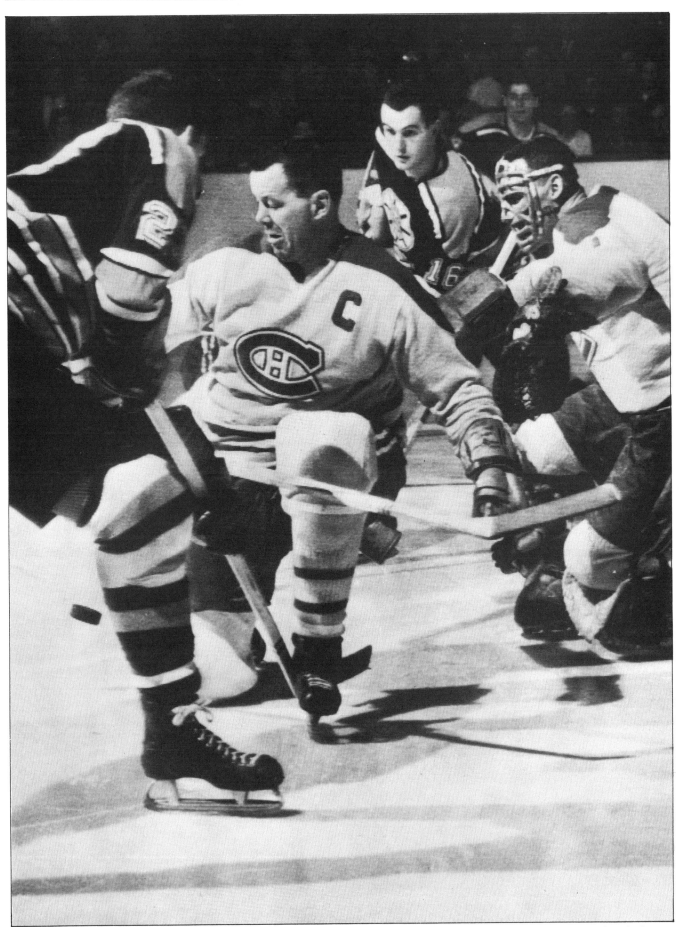

Doug Harvey comes to the aid of Plante

that the league changed the rule and allowed the offending player to return to the ice before his two minutes were up if a power-play goal was scored. Otherwise Montreal might pop in three or four.

On the other hand, the Canadiens were long favored by a league rule that gave them first crack at the best two francophone hockey players available.

That disappeared with the advent of the universal draft. As a result, there are as many American players with Montreal today as French-speaking Canadiens. To compensate, the teams' front office has become almost entirely French-speaking for the first time in team history, from president Ronald Corey on down to coach Jean Perron.

Dreaming of the Stanley Cup— gone since 1979, the longest hiatus since the dark days of 1945–46 through 1952–53—is back in fashion. Guy Lafleur, the Demon Blond, is gone, but for the first time in a long time another crop of flying Frenchmen looms on the horizon: forwards Stephan Richer, Claude Lemieux, Joze Charbonneau, Sergion Momesso and goalie Patrick Roy.

If the Canadiens have been rebuilding their image in recent years, much of the blame or credit can go to the Quebec Nordiques, their new rivals from down Highway 40, who eliminated them from playoff competition twice in four years.

The Canadiens' owner, La Brasserie Molson, has responded with

vigor, put some good people in the right places, and the product has been selling well.

This is primarily because most of the good burghers of the province, outside the immediate environs of Quebec City, have remained faithful to "their" team with a ferocious attachment, visceral, sentimental, exclusive. It is a story of impassioned love where logic has no role to play. But then again, isn't it said that love is blind?

Montreal is the best and worst place to play hockey. The Forum is the sport's mecca. Rookies are over-

A winning combination: Jean Beliveau, Jacques Plante, Toe Blake and Boom-Boom Geoffrion celebrate clinching the NHL championship in 1961

whelmed on arrival and every Canadien is recognized in the street, even the bit players. The pressure is unbelievable. The sports pages of the French-language dailies routinely print dozens of daily hockey articles and the major radio stations feature sports hotlines, where fans manage the team, make trades and fire players and coaches on the air.

When the Canadiens travel, an impressive media entourage goes with them, including reporters from all the dailies, English and French radio and television crews, even radio talk-show hosts.

Ronald Corey puts it succinctly: ''The Canadiens are not allowed to lose; the fans won't have it.''

The reason for the Canadiens'

dynasty is easy to understand: the pressure from the fans forces them to surpass themselves. They are a team with three million owners and at least as many coaches.

How can they lose?

Below: Some of the 22 Stanley Cup banners
hanging from the roof of The Forum

Overleaf: Ken Dryden

Photography Credits